How the West End Became the West End

A Deep Dive Into the History of London's Theater Scene

Isaac Q. Miller

© Copyright 2024 - **All rights reserved.**

The content contained within this book may not be reproduced, duplicated or transmitted without direct written permission from the author or the publisher.

Under no circumstances will any blame or legal responsibility be held against the publisher, or author, for any damages, reparation, or monetary loss due to the information contained within this book, either directly or indirectly.

Legal Notice:

This book is copyright protected. It is only for personal use. You cannot amend, distribute, sell, use, quote or paraphrase any part, or the content within this book, without the consent of the author or publisher.

Disclaimer Notice:

Please note the information contained within this document is for educational and entertainment purposes only. All effort has been executed to present accurate, up to date, reliable, complete information. No warranties of any kind are declared or implied. Readers acknowledge that the author is not engaged in the rendering of legal, financial, medical or professional advice. The content within this book has been derived from various sources. Please consult a licensed professional before attempting any techniques outlined in this book.

By reading this document, the reader agrees that under no circumstances is the author responsible for any losses, direct or indirect, that are incurred as a result of the use of the information contained within this document, including, but not limited to, errors, omissions, or inaccuracies.

Join My Newsletter!

Click here or scan the QR code to join my newsletter, stay informed on all things theater, the West End, and more!

Introduction

The first time I went to London, I made the genius decision that I didn't need to see any theatrical shows while I was there. In fact, I'm embarrassed to say that even though I'm a huge Broadway fan, I didn't even know what the equivalent was in London. This was despite knowing that shows on Broadway often end up in London or are directly from London (hello, *Mamma Mia*).

I decided that since I see plenty of shows in New York every year, I should put my time into seeing all the other sights and landmarks I could find—big mistake.

I walked through London's West End streets by accident, and I couldn't believe my eyes. Don't get me wrong. I'm not saying that London's West End is better than Broadway. Honestly, there's no point in comparing them. Instead, any theater buff—like me—can enjoy these two places on Earth that are the closest to paradise. It is remarkable how much Broadway and the West End have in common and, at the same time, are so different.

My group and I landed at Piccadilly Circus, where we were supposed to spend a couple of hours in the area until

Introduction

the bus picked us up to go to the British Museum. We started walking and found many impressive buildings that merged classic architecture with neon lights. I ran into several theater billboards with so many familiar names on them, including many I had never heard of before.

I was impressed by the varied offers of stage productions: musicals, comedy, drama, and even some old classics. It was like a journey around the world and into the past. I ended up buying a ticket for a show for each night left of my time in London.

Before leaving London, I was already booking my next trip. I needed to return and see some of the plays I'd discovered.

After returning to my minuscule apartment in New York, I started reading and learning everything I could about London's West End. It has an incredible history that merges with European history and contemporary culture, especially regarding performing arts.

London's West End is the cultural district of one of the most important capitals in the world. It is located in Central London, in a vaguely defined area west of the City of London and north of the River Thames. It includes many famous attractions such as palaces, public offices, monuments, and shops that captivate tourists and locals alike. Visitors can find 39 theaters offering theatrical shows to suit anyone's taste.

The West End is the place where theater happens. It's the cradle of contemporary performing arts. The history of theater in London's West End is deeply linked to the evolution of Western culture. Its influence has crossed back and forth across the Atlantic Ocean and built a unique parallel with Broadway. Together, they have laid the foundations of theater.

Introduction

In this book, I will focus on the West End's unique contribution to the development of performing arts in England, in Europe, and across the globe.

London's West End has been through a long and eventful evolution that started many centuries ago when the Romans reached Great Britain. We will explore the roots of the Roman legacy that was left behind and so much more.

Throughout these chapters, we will unveil the most relevant moments in the history of London's West End. The theater has had its ups and downs accompanying social, economic, and political changes. It also became one of the leading resources for society to flourish. At present, it continues to reflect and inspire cultural movements and promote the evolution of society.

Curtains up, and let the show begin!

Chapter 1

Origins of London Theater

London was once the capital of a Roman province. It was built in the image and likeness of many other Roman cities in the Empire. Early Londoners' lives were shaped by Roman culture.

Within the Roman Empire, the theater and public spectacles were in part meant for entertainment—but played a unique role in their social and political system. The theater was a space where emperors built the legitimacy of their reign since, there, Roman citizens experienced a sense of power and equality among themselves despite their differences in status.

Roman Influences and Early Performances

In ancient times, the Romans had spread their power and influence throughout the world, including Great Britain. For three and a half centuries, Britannia was a Roman province. Therefore, the impact and influence of Roman culture in London and the United Kingdom is extensive and deep-rooted (Pattison, n.d.).

London would never be the same after the arrival of the Romans. Even though the people didn't elect Roman officials, they knew social peace was the basis of political stability and progress. Therefore, they dedicated time and money to keeping the crowd entertained and happy. With that purpose, they created a number of public spectacles that were used to deliver political propaganda and to provide the people with a space to express themselves.

In ancient Rome, the state controlled the entertainment industry to manipulate the public into supporting the rulers' interests. Magnificent amphitheaters for audiences of hundreds of thousands of people were built in the most important cities, along with public baths, circuses, and gymnasiums. The Colosseum in Rome, the capital of the Empire, is the most worldwide recognized arena from ancient Rome, but it wasn't the only one.

The amphitheaters were inspired by the Greek theater. They were open-air buildings with the shape of an ellipse. They were placed on natural slopes to give the spectators a good view of the space where the actors were performing. The raised seats were usually rocks from the hills. Others had wooden seats, which were much more comfortable for the enthusiastic spectators.

The type of spectacle displayed in the building determined the amphitheater's shape. Circuses and stadiums were rectangular and prepared for races and sports competitions. Arenas, instead, were designed for people to enjoy live combat among gladiators (which usually ended in death), *venationes* (combats that included animals), and executions. A particular type of gladiator combat consisted of dramatizing famous battles (Milligan, 2016). During the bloody mock gladiators' shows, they confronted the imperial army, always representing the part of the defeated enemy.

The Roman amphitheater in *Londinium* (London in Latin) was located by the Thames River, where the Guildhall Art Gallery was built. The ruins were discovered while making the gallery in 1988, almost 2,000 years after the amphitheater opened. The latter was built when London was already an active harbor for luxury goods trading (City of London, n.d.).

The presentations in London's amphitheater were violent spectacles, but thousands attended them. There, they didn't behave like civilized individuals but as part of an unrestrained crowd (City of London, n.d.). This concept of entertainment seems incomprehensible from a contemporary perspective. Nonetheless, it is possible to find violence and rage in the entertainment business. Perhaps the main and fundamental difference is that energy is now funneled into fictional productions.

Street Performances and Traveling Troupes

After the Romans withdrew, the Jutes, Angles, and Saxons —Germanic tribes from northern Europe—arrived in Britain. They subjugated the local Celtic population and installed Roman-Germanic kingdoms, similar to what happened in the rest of Europe. Those kingdoms evolved and shaped the Middle Ages' lifestyle. Roman Britannia then changed to *Angleland*, which is closer to the present-day name, England (Daileader, 2020).

After the Romans' withdrawal, theaters and other public spectacles declined. The Roman theaters fell into ruin. However, the new lifestyles in the medieval villages accompanied the evolution of performing arts in different spaces: streets.

During the Middle Ages, most of the population were

peasants and lived in the countryside. The castles where the feudal lords lived and the monasteries were the centers of political power and where the whole village sheltered in times of war. High fortifications were built to protect the people from foreign invasions, especially from the Vikings (Symes, 2023). Within the walls of the fortifications, towns started to grow.

The towns that developed beyond the walls became the trade market for the peasants and the space for merchants and laborers of different offices to settle their businesses. They placed their market stalls in the streets, and the community gathered there. Most parts of public life happened in the market in medieval society. Once or twice a year, big fairs were carried out in the bigger towns, and people from neighboring villages came to trade goods.

Art performers played an essential role in medieval society. In England, in particular, they even had a political responsibility. The landlord hired musicians to guard the town entrance. If an enemy approached, musicians played loud enough to warn everybody (Gioia, 2022). Yet, art performances were generally associated with pagan practices and, therefore, looked down upon by the guardians of morality. Jesting, dancing, and other types of performances endured despite the momentary disappearance of theater but were considered sinful activities.

Despite the lack of sufficient written evidence of art performers in medieval Europe, it is known that there were many different street performers who amused people while shopping in the street markets. These artists were professionals in that they earned a living by exhibiting their talents and creativity. They can all be encompassed in the general term "jesters." They were singers, mime artists, tightrope walkers, puppeteers, acrobats, jugglers, musicians, jesters, animal trainers, and fortune tellers, to name a few (Carlson, 2013; Pietrini, 2010).

A typical medieval street performer was the shadow puppeteer. They represented theatrical plays through shadows projected by puppets behind a curtain. These flourished in the Arabic world and were introduced to Europe during the Middle Ages. Their scripts recreated environments where the characters interacted through dialogue, and the plot's action followed a storyline similar to present-day theater plays (Carlson, 2013).

The jugglers and acrobats performed their acts, and then their masters or assistants would appear to ask the audience to make some contributions. These characters emphasized the risks and skills deployed to entertain them and, therefore, deserved compensation (Carlson, 2013). This is similar to contemporary street artists nowadays.

Fortune tellers had their own routine. They settled their stuff in a spot and asked one or two audience members to come forward. The fortune teller read their horoscope before an astounded audience (Carlson, 2013). It isn't clear if the invitees were also actors and the presentation was set in advance or if they were spontaneous volunteers.

In the Late Middle Ages, the troubadours emerged as a new type of performer. They can be distinguished from these street performers who sold their rudimentary art in the streets at cheap prices. The troubadours composed verses and songs they performed with musical instruments to tell stories of knights and epic battles. Instead of performing in the streets, they went from one village to another and performed in castles and private banquets. They belonged to a higher class of art performers and played a different societal role. They entertained and educated the audience about important historical characters and events (Pietrini, 2010).

As trading increased, the importance of cities grew, as did the crossroads of the main trading routes. The roads that led to London were surrounded by inns and taverns for travelers to rest and eat. These places became the new spaces for theatrical presentations. Even though street artists didn't disappear, the inns became the new center of performing arts.

The population grew in the cities, and so did the audiences for the performances in the inns. The government of London attempted to ban this activity due to the high level of havoc it caused. People in the inns got drunk and exhibited immoral behavior (Londonist, 2022). As the potential theatrical audiences grew, so did the possibilities for running a new business. However, the evolution of theater in London was carried out by religious institutions with a strict moralizing purpose—this would play an essential role in the theater's history.

Influence of Medieval Religious Plays

After the Roman Empire fell, Christianity declined in Britain during the following centuries. However, the Church regained power as the medieval society developed. Between the 10th and 13th centuries, the Catholic Church doubled its efforts to explain the new faith to a population that was primarily pagan.

In England, as in most parts of Western Europe, early theaters evolved through the initiative of church services. The local religious community presented passages from the Bible and the life of saints on particular days of the year. While the priest prayed in Latin, the plays performed on those occasions were in the vernacular language so everybody in the audience could understand (V&A, n.d.). It was an effective way to educate the illiterate masses in Christian doctrine and engage them in daily religious practices.

The theatrical presentations were displayed on special religious festivities such as *Corpus Christi*, Easter, and Christmas. Also, on many occasions, there were large fairs organized by the guilds of merchants and artisans. There, people from nearby towns and the travelers who arrived with the caravan traders gathered to participate in the fair and the religious celebration. Religious processions were carried out and ended in a theatrical presentation of "mystery cycles."

These mystery cycles were short plays covering certain Bible passages, mainly from the Old Testament. Along a procession, more than one cycle was presented. There were stages at different points of the path where each cycle was represented.

These plays delivered a moral message. The Catholic Church used them to talk to the audience about the salvation of humankind through their religion. They usually began with Adam and Eve's story in the Garden of Eden; the image of Satan tempting them to disobey God and sin was very vividly represented. In the consecutive stories, the performers represented moments of Jesus Christ's life to show the citizens that salvation was possible thanks to his sacrifice. The parade ended with Jesus Christ's crucifixion and resurrection (Soergel, n.d.).

Some of these mystery cycles were particularly violent; for instance, the representation of Jesus' torture, the beheading of John the Baptist by Herod Antipas, or the torment of saints and martyrs. The actors deployed techniques and resources to give the performance more realism.

They had a way of imitating blood to make a greater impression on the audience. However, these moments were alternated with comic scenes to ease the play's tone.

Besides passages from the Bible, the productions also depicted miracles and the lives of saints and martyrs. They were called "miracle plays," and the most frequent were those of the Virgin Mary and Saint Nicholas. The narratives were meant to seed faith in miracles and the belief that a life of surrender to God's will would achieve salvation in the people's minds (StudySmarter, n.d.).

These plays are considered early forms of dramatic presentations, as they encompass several elements of drama. For instance, they involved dialogues among the performers who embodied characters. These plays were called "liturgical dramas," and, in addition to the actors' expositions, they had an introduction and a conclusion to guide the audience in properly understanding the message (StudySmarter, n.d.). Within the development of the act, there was also a voice that intervened with explanations and transitions from one scene to another.

As explained, these theatrical presentations were performed in a variety of buildings. Instead, several stages called mansions were mounted along the procession's path. In England, pageant wagons carried these mansions to different points in the city, and the artists performed the same cycle several times (Soergel, n.d.).

It is interesting to know that these mystery cycle plays were periodically held and scheduled. Since it was essential to keep the audience informed about future presentations, banners announcing them were hung in public places such as markets and squares.

These fairs or religious festivities were important events for medieval people. They represented moments of more intense cultural and economic activity. Stages were placed outside the Church, and the performers were essentially local artists. The guilds hired carpenters, sculptors, and painters to prepare the stage and the scenography.

The processions and fairs played an essential role in the towns and cities. They summoned countless local people and visitors and became an element of civic pride as they helped develop the national identity.

The importance of mystery cycles declined after the Protestant Reformation and during the religious conflicts in Europe between the 15th and 16th centuries. In England, Protestantism was made the official religion, and mystery cycles were restricted. Despite the original educational purpose of medieval religious plays, they set the foundations of dramatic performances as a viable industry of entertainment (StudySmarter, n.d.).

The Influence of Roman Mythology on Early Theater

During the 1,000 years that the Middle Ages lasted, the interest in Roman and ancient culture was first replaced by the merging of the local culture with that of the Germanic tribes that invaded the territories of what had been the Roman Empire. Later, the Catholic Church increased its power and soon became the most distinctive element of the medieval mindset. Religious themes dominated the theatrical presentation and had a solid indoctrinating purpose.

Since the 15th century, Europe entered an era of deep cultural turbulence and change. The cities flourished, and the wealth enabled by colonial expansion and international trading gave people new perspectives on life. It eventually led to a significant cultural change. Science and arts reemerged and challenged the power of the Church, which also had to face the Protestant Reformation. The sense of morality, beauty, and goodness changed. The human being became the center of interest, and there was renewed attention to the ancient Greek and Roman heritage.

In the 15th century, political, social, economic, and cultural changes brought about the rebirth of the Classic Ages. The printing press rapidly propagated the new ideas. This cultural movement was called the Renaissance and inspired artists and writers from all over Europe. They adapted the Greek and Roman myths to their current social environment to improve society (Carpintero Diez, 2015).

Even though the religious themes didn't completely disappear from the artistic manifestations, including performing arts, the main topics reflected the Classical Age. Therefore, the new plays were adaptations of Greek myths and legends, and the stories were about the Roman gods and goddesses, who are, in fact, the Roman version of the Greek pantheon.

In a sense, the purpose of theater continued to be moralizing and educational. Greco-Roman mythology wasn't conveyed as a religious doctrine, but myths still had a high focus on morality. They were a reflection of deep human attributes. Gods and goddesses were an idealized representation of human traits, and they promoted certain values among others, such as courage, discipline, obedience, and reason over sensitivity and impulsivity.

Greek and Roman mythology was usually relayed in Latin, enabling a universal circulation of the ideas. However, this circulation was targeted only at educated people. Writers had the mission to write about innovative ideas in the vernacular languages to let these ideas reach ordinary people.

There were two main ways to include Greek and Roman myths and characters. The writers could use the core of the myth and its profound meaning to create a brand-new story. Others used the characters as external references that more informed audiences could interpret. Many plays combined both methods in original pieces that provided people with a new framework to understand the human condition and the world around them (Carpintero Diez, 2015).

The Renaissance brought many changes in Europe, particularly in England, where it boosted the evolution of theater. It was enabled by political power and royals sensitive to artistic manifestations.

Chapter 2
The Renaissance of London Theater

Between the 15th and 16th centuries, Europe entered a period of transition between the Late Middle Ages and modernity. The process of change involved economic, political, and social aspects and caused a drastic cultural turn in Europeans' mindset.

The Catholic church lost power in front of the advancement of secular power in the new states ruled by absolute monarchs. This had a tremendous cultural impact. In the economic aspect, lucrative purposes of searching for success in business replaced the medieval ideal of austerity and the final goal of eternal salvation after death. Reason and science replaced faith in miracles and God's power over human beings' destinies. A whole new conception of humanity arose, and that, of course, was replicated in art.

Science and the arts flourish in societies that reach periods of growth and expansion. The Renaissance coincided with the consolidation of princes' and monarchs' powers. There were also social changes: a new social class, the bourgeoisie, emerged and became wealthy enough to make bold investments in non-essential activities. The population in the cities increased, and people experienced a new daily life that wasn't limited to producing their own means of survival.

In England, the Renaissance began with the Tudor Dynasty at the end of the 1400s. They unified the kingdom under the power of one absolute monarch and ruled for over a century. It reached the cultural summit when the last Tudor came to power. Elizabeth I, Henry VIII's second heir to the crown, ruled between 1558 and 1603 and became a charismatic leader with a special care for the arts.

During the Tudors' reign, England became a global power with an unyielding empire conquering lands across the globe and dominating the seas economically and militarily. The printing press enabled the diffusion of new ideas, and literacy grew among the population. London became the biggest city in Europe, with thriving ports and markets—the perfect frame for developing theaters (Poetry Foundation, n.d.).

The Renaissance Theater in England

In England, theater flourished during the Renaissance. The period lasted between the religious Reformation and the closure of theaters due to the political turmoil during the Puritan Revolution in 1642. The performance of the play *The Tragedie of Gorboduc* in 1562 is considered the beginning of the period (StudySmarter, n.d.).

Renaissance theater retrieved many elements from medieval presentations. However, new ideas were reflected in the themes of the plays. The mystery cycles were replaced first by morality plays and adaptations of the

Greek and Roman myths called university drama. Nonetheless, the people in charge of the theatrical productions were profoundly changed.

In the Middle Ages, the producers were people of the church and the local guilds. In the Renaissance, the theater became a profitable activity, and private entrepreneurs held plays with the pursuit of providing entertainment and earning a profit. At the end of the 1400s, some guild productions still competed against the new private companies. In the 1500s, the theater was predominantly professional and managed by companies. These companies were self-governed, and many were cooperative, dividing the revenues among all the crew members.

This organization of the companies enabled the professionalization of acting. While in the past, the actors had been local people who performed only for special occasions, during the Renaissance, professional artists emerged. That means that their regular incomes came from acting, and they did it as a full-time activity. For a while, a particular rivalry existed between actors who belonged to the guilds and the new professional performers.

The actors were all men, mostly young, who generally played several roles in a play. Women were not accepted in theatrical companies—as happened in most public life spaces—and men would perform female characters. The company hired temporary actors for specific plays, always for minor characters. The leading roles were preserved for the regular members of the company.

Playwrights emerged and increased, as they could earn money by writing the plays. They were also exclusively men. Some of them had an academic background, even though most of them came from the lower classes. Theater and playwriting soon became a way of social promotion. However, the play's author didn't keep the rights to his work. Instead, it belonged to the company that bought it.

Despite the flourishing business, the development of theater and performing artists wasn't easy. These actors were autonomous artists who made a living but didn't belong to any formal institutions. They weren't members of a craftsman guild. In 1572, the Government of London passed a new law that labeled them as vagabonds charged with prison sentences. To protect themselves, actors and companies had to put themselves under the protection of a patron.

Patrons were nobles with high social status. Sometimes, they gave the artists economic resources, but the most important was the public support for people who otherwise were outside the law. This situation eventually changed when Queen Elizabeth I, an enthusiast of theater and arts, allowed theaters to open once more and recognized acting as a legal profession.

Soon, theaters multiplied in the cities, and the number of plays created increased. Many plays were held at universities by students, usually on Greco-Roman topics. Plays were rehearsed and performed for the royal court in front of the Queen and then were presented in front of the public. By then, royalty and ordinary people attended the same plays. Later, under the reign of Charles I, private theaters became popular, and special plays were written for the upper class. Other plays were presented in public playhouses for the common people.

The theatrical performances were mainly presented in the palaces and courts of noblemen, and the companies also used to travel from town to town with their plays. From the last decades of the 15th century, theaters emerged as venues built for the specific purpose of hosting theatrical presentations. These theaters were public places, and people had to pay a fee to attend the plays.

The Opening of the First Public Theater

The first public theater in London opened in 1567. It was called the Red Lion, but it didn't last long. The next theater opened a year later. It was simply called "The Theater" and this one *is* considered to be London's first permanent theater. It was built by the owner of the Red Lion and his brother-in-law in 1576. It was located in the East End of present-day London. It became popular after William Shakespeare performed there several times.

The Newington Butts Playhouse was also one of the first theaters in London, though there isn't enough information to know the exact year it was built. It happened at some time between 1575 and 1577. It was located near the Thames River on the southern end of London, where the city had yet to spread. It remained open for about 20 years. It is fair to assume that it was difficult for people to get there because it was so far from the city center (Nicol, n.d.).

The Theater and the Newington Butts were followed by the Curtain Theater, which opened in 1577. In the following years, the Rose, the Swan, the Globe, the Fortune, and the Red Bull also opened in chronological order between 1587 and 1604 (Lumen Learning, n.d.). They were all outside the city in the area neighboring Southwark. All of them were reasonably close to each other but far enough from the public office to stay out of the council's control, which had attempted to ban the activity (Cliffnotes, n.d.).

How the West End Became the West End

Between 1576 and 1597, the Blackfriars Theatre also opened. The building used to be a monastery, and during Elizabeth I's reign, it was assigned to the Children of Chapel, who rehearsed and performed for the court. In 1596, the owner of the Theater, James Burbage, bought a part of the Blackfriars and made a significant investment to transform it into a private playhouse. Burbage's son was an actor in William Shakespeare's company called the Chamberlain's Men, and in 1597, the company inherited the theater (Best et al., 2002). It remained open until 1655, when it was demolished.

The emergence of so many theaters in a relatively short period was related to the appearance of several theatrical companies and the increase in the popularity of theatrical presentations. The opening of public playhouses accompanied and boosted this evolution and popularity.

All theaters built in this period were open air to use daylight for most performances. If night came before the play ended, they would light up candles to let the actors finish the presentation. Most theaters were built in a polygonal shape with a space in the middle where the stage was set. Most of them were oval to improve the sound quality and enable everybody in the audience to listen to the actors' voices. However, the Red Bull and the Fortune were squares. In all of them, the distance between the audience and the performers was considerably small.

The sides had three stories with different levels of seats to give all audience members a proper view of the stage. They were galleries with seats, all looking at the stage on three sides. The fourth side was left for the musicians who played live and the actors to enter and leave the stage. The location of the seat meant a different fee regarding the quality of the sight it provided. There were also reserved seats for the wealthiest of the community that were placed separated from the crowd. The seats closer to the stage or in these privileged locations were more expensive.

The Globe was quite particular. It was an octagon with a trap door under the floor of the stage. During the show, actors representing ghosts and specters could make a magical appearance in front of the audience (Cliffnotes, n.d.).

The theaters were built to hold thousands of people. In 1580, all the theaters of London could host about 5,000 spectators. This number doubled by 1610 as the theatrical companies multiplied and the audience expanded.

The building of theaters and the emergence of more companies were significant during the last decades of the 16th century and the beginning of the 17th century. However, they faced more than one challenge. On the one hand, London authorities prohibited plays because they alleged their content had immoral arguments, but there were other reasons, such as sanitation. In the 1570s and the beginning of the 1600s, the Bubonic Plague (the Great Plague) ravaged the city and killed thousands of Londoners. Therefore, theaters had to cancel the functions.

In addition to these circumstances, the theater was perceived as challenging social order and political power. It was considered subversive (Rasmussen & DeJong, 2017). In 1597, the London council attempted to close the theater where the play *The Isle of Dogs* by Thomas Nashe and Ben Jonson was performed. It was a satirical play that questioned or ridiculed the local authorities and, therefore, was condemned for being seditious.

The council wanted to close all theaters as an exemplary punishment, but Queen Elizabeth, once more, intervened to preserve the artists. It is fair to assume the Queen was well aware of the influence the theater could have on people, but she also supported it as another element of the changes taking place under her reign (Rasmussen & DeJong, 2017).

Shakespeare's Early Works and Collaborations

Undoubtedly, William Shakespeare is one of the most renowned playwrights of the Elizabethan theater and the epitome of the dramatic genre. Even though he had a prolific life and presented many of his plays in London during the Elizabethan era, his prestige in his country and abroad would rise even further in the 19th century when playwrights and directors adapted his original plays to make them more relatable for audiences.

What is known by historians about his early life has a lot of blanks and is filled with conjectures that lack solid or convincing evidence. It is known that he was born in Stratford-upon-Avon in 1564 and arrived in London sometime before 1592. That was the first time his name appeared in any document in London's history (Bevington et al., 2023). It is believed, however, that his job as a playwright began some years later. He wrote most of his plays, at least those that have transcended fame, between 1589 and 1613 (Elizabethan Era, n.d.).

His reputation began to grow after the time of the plague. Before that, he worked for several companies, but after 1594, he joined the Lord Chamberlain's Men company. It was under Lord Chamberlain's patronage during this time, and Richard Burbage, the theater's owner's son, was the starring actor. The company soon became the most prestigious in London. When Queen Elizabeth died, King James I replaced her on the throne and became the new patron of the company, which then became called the King's Men.

At first, Shakespeare's plays were performed in the theater until the company also bought the Globe, which actually opened for the owner's son to star in his company's plays. It gathered people from all social classes for their afternoon presentations, but they also performed at the court for the Queen and nobility. The Lord Chamberlain's Men performed in front of 3,000 people. Later, the owner also bought the Blackfriars Theatre.

Shakespeare started writing historical plays and comedies about the lives of kings. Then, he also wrote tragedies. Among his early plays, it is worth naming *Henry VI* (the three parts), *Titus Andronicus*, and *Three Gentlemen of Verona* (Shakespeare Birthplace Trust, n.d.). The order in which he wrote them remains unknown.

Later, his professional production was divided into four groups: romance, comedy, history, and tragedy. He wrote about several issues: love, revenge, historical characters and events, and murder. He also adapted several elements from the ancient Greek tragedy; for instance, *Romeo and Juliet* is probably Shakespeare's most famous play in the present. Also, *A Midsummer Night's Dream* tells the story of the romance between the Greek hero Theseus and the Amazon Hippolyte. The latter was Shakespeare's most famous play of his time (Cartwright, 2020).

Shakespeare's work was loved by many but also rejected by the most conservative sectors of London society: Puritans and their followers. Like many other authors' works, his plays were perceived as pernicious. Like *The Isle of the*

Dogs, Shakespeare's plays about the kings' lives (*Richard III* and *Henry V*) were questioned for picturing unpopular profiles of the monarchs, which could be seen as against national integrity. Shakespeare and his company wouldn't have endured without the direct support of Queen Elizabeth.

Like most playwrights of his time, Shakespeare collaborated with other writers. He wrote the three parts of *King Henry VI* in collaboration with Cristopher Marlowe. This and Marlowe's own work were considered a series of antipatriotic plays (Rasmussen & DeJong, 2017). This had a great impact on Shakespeare's later writings. In the works known as the "great tragedies" (*Macbeth, Hamlet, Othello,* and *King Lear*), the main themes revolve around political conflicts and an underlying questioning of the relationship between monarchs and subjects.

Subversive Drama Playwrights

As mentioned before, the theater was a sign of the changes that were taking place in England during the last part of the 16th century. It reflected society and, at the same time, helped shape it under the new mindset. For many conservative people in power, secular and religious, this was resisted and feared.

By then, playwrights who defied the government's request to produce patriotic plays with a moralizing message were considered subversive. Christopher Marlowe was one of those writers. In addition to a controversial personal life that found him mixed into occasional scandals, Marlowe chose to write about whatever could amuse the multitude, soon becoming very popular.

Isaac Q. Miller

Christopher Marlowe and John Webster's Revenge Tragedies

Tragedy is one of the two formative genres of theater. During the English Renaissance, tragic drama focused on revenge stories and their fatal consequences. The genre flourished in the 1600s after Queen Elizabeth's death and during King James' reign. One of the most famous plays was Thomas Kyd's *The Spanish Tragedy*, in which the characters kill and commit suicide because of jealousy. This play was written and premiered before *Romeo and Juliet*. Shakespeare also wrote several revenge tragedies: *Hamlet* is a remarkable example of the genre where the prince of Denmark searched for revenge on his uncle Claudius.

Christopher Marlowe was particularly popular for his tragedies and revenge dramas. His plays were performed by the Queen's Men, a company under the patronage of the Queen herself. Therefore, Marlowe was compelled to produce plays that served political goals. He was asked to write English nationalistic plays framed in Puritan morals. However, Marlowe couldn't help introducing his rebellious insight even in his most conventional writings. For instance, *Doctor Faustus*, one of his most famous plays, conveyed a moral tale, but he managed to question the legitimacy of that moral background (Rasmussen & DeJong, 2017).

Marlowe's *The Massacre at Paris* started as a condemnation of the French and the Catholics, directly aligned with English national interest. However, the play expertly changed and turned out to be a reflection of the country's political reality.

Marlowe had a moment of glory when he was considered a celebrity. He even belonged to Queen Elizabeth's secret service. Nonetheless, things didn't end well. His roommate, Thomas Kyd, was accused of immoral behavior due to the tone of his plays. It is believed that Kyd confessed under torture that Marlowe had written his plays.

Marlowe was prosecuted for heresy and died in unclear circumstances. It is argued that he was executed by a secret mission of the royal services. He was buried in a tomb with no name (Encyclopedia.com, n.d.).

In Marlowe and Shakespeare's tragedies, revenge is motivated by a sense of honor. It was a moral duty to take revenge on those who had caused damage. That perception of revenge changed in John Webster's plays. Webster told stories where revenge was an act of immoral people. Avengers were villains who searched not for justice but for personal satisfaction.

Webster's renowned plays were violent and macabre stories based on true-life facts. The plays were *The White Devil* (1612) and *The Duchess of Malfi* (1614), both set in Italy. The first one was performed in the Red Bull Theater and is about the assassination of a gentlewoman. The second is Webster's most celebrated play. It's about two vengeful brothers who kill their sister for marrying a man below their class (Royal Shakespeare Company, n.d.).

Ben Jonson's Comedic Plays and Satires—The 'War of the Theaters'

When theater emerged in ancient Greece, tragedy was meant to teach the citizens to obey the rules of deities and state cities. Therefore, comedy was used as a means of political criticism. During the Elizabethan era, comedy developed as a subgenre within drama.

Influenced by the Roman New Comedy, Ovidian comedy emerged as a subtype. It mainly targeted the illiterate sectors of society and covered domestic issues instead of targeting critics against public characters from politics (Porter, 2022). Some of the most famous were *The Shoemaker's Holiday*, written by Thomas Dekker, and *A Chaste Maid in Cheapside*, by Thomas Middleton.

Unlike the other genres, Ovidian comedy didn't pursue any moral purpose. Instead, the plays were about myths and contained a high charge of erotism that scandalized the Puritans and conservatives who broadly rejected these infamous plays.

Besides the Ovidian comedy, another subgenre also emerged: satires. These plays made people laugh not only because funny events were performed but also because the prose and the lyrics were hilarious. The plays aimed to ridicule the prominent characters and expose the corruption of society. Satires played a role in political expression.

Ben Jonson is the leading representative of satires. He came from a marginal place in society but searched for the high-class members' patronage. Therefore, he targeted his plays at the gallant people of London society, though sometimes, the content of his plays was about ridiculing them for the things he disapproved of. However, he aimed to improve his audience through his plays; thus, he used satire to achieve his moralizing purpose. Nowadays, Jonson's most famous plays are *Volpone* and *The Alchemist*, both of which satirize greed (Kiney, 2004). In his time, some of the most renowned plays were *Every Man Out of His Humour* and *Cynthia's Revels*, two plays of social vindication of the poor conditions of poets and playwrights in London society. Despite Johnson's intention, those plays eventually led to the so-called 'War of the Theatres' (Kay, 1995).

The conflict unfolded between Johnson and another two playwrights, John Marston and Thomas Dekker. The three of them used the characters of their plays to attack each other. It isn't clear if Jonson's plays triggered the conflict or if his characters were an answer to Marston. It is also controversial to decide if it was a genuine rivalry between playwrights and the companies or just a means of propaganda to sell more tickets (Literature Guide, 2020). Elizabethan theater laid the grounds for contemporary theater in so many ways!

Influence on Improvisation and Physical Comedy

Elizabethan comedy received great influence from the Italian *commedia dell'arte*. This type of theater emerged in Italy and flourished in Europe during the 16th century, reaching England in the 1570s. *Commedia dell'arte* consisted of plays with open scripts and allowed the actors to improvise parts of the dialogues and actions. They were performed by traveling troupes that eventually visited different countries in Europe. These plays were about failed love stories, helpful or dull servants, and authoritarian parents (Gay, 2016).

This type of comedy allowed improvisation and physical performance by amateur and professional actors. They added masks and colorful costumes to their presentations. These masks and costumes allowed the actors to create well-defined characters. Even though they improvised throughout the performance, the characters were fixed and generally represented in opposed pairs (the rich and the poor, the male and the female, and so on). There were four families of characters: the elderly, the *Zanni* (the servants), the lovers, and the *Capitano*. The latter was an unfriendly character who represented a pretentious military man (Encyclopaedia Britannica, 2023a).

Servants and low-class workers performed physical clowning comedies, and some of the most frequent themes were the battle between the sexes. It was also a transition between medieval theater that had focused on mystery cycles and modern theater. Comedians presented scenes or fragments from the Bible, but the plot was a battle between male and female characters; for instance, an argument between Noah and his wife before entering the arch (Gay, 2016).

In England, improvisation and physical comedy significantly influenced Shakespeare's plays. The best examples of this comedy style are *The Taming of the Shrew* and *The Merchant of Venice*. In these plays, Shakespeare included characters that wore masks to depict the characters, and all the stereotypical characters of the *commedia dell'arte* can be identified in *The Taming of the Shrew*.

Historical and Patriotic Plays

The third theatrical genre that developed in the Elizabethan era was historical plays. It is difficult to define it as a unique genre because it encompasses several different plays. The central theme of these plays was related to English history. Most of the plays had the name of a king in their title (Obermajerová, 2011).

It isn't strange that the genre evolved almost simultaneously with the consolidation of the national state under the power of the monarchs. Theaters played a critical political role in the standardization of the use of language and, at the same time, created a cultural frame where every citizen could feel included. Historical plays helped shape the national identity, strengthening the bonds between the citizens and the nation based on a glorious and heroic shared past.

The stories about the kings were meant to build an image of a leader with power based not only on a divine design but also on popular support. Historical plays were supposed to reinforce the power of the monarchs by building legitimacy among the citizen spectators. Other recurrent topics were famous battles that were landmarks in recent history. This was also used to exacerbate national pride and demonize the enemies.

Historical plays also had an educational purpose. It was a way for the lower illiterate classes to learn about the country's history. However, these plays were only sometimes based on scholarly research. Instead, the playwrights told fictional stories about real historical characters, usually retrieving components of folk plays (Obermajerová, 2011; No Sweat Shakespeare, n.d.). Historical veracity wasn't the primary concern, indeed. Besides, although the main characters were mainly monarchs, all social classes were represented in historical plays.

William Shakespeare's early plays can be classified as historical plays: *King John, Richard II, Henry IV, Henry V, Richard III,* and *Henry VIII.* In these plays, Shakespeare exposed the rivalry between the English and the French in the Middle Ages and the War of the Two Roses that ended up with the kingdom's unification and the Tudors' arrival to the throne.

The golden age of theater was enabled by the favor of the Tudor monarchs, who extensively used it to benefit their power. Culture flourished, and political stability endured. This golden age would reach its downfall along with the Tudors. In 1642, political turmoil brought new changes to England—changes that seemed to take everything backward. The Puritans gained control in London, and a civil war began.

Chapter 3

Theaters and Performers in the Restoration Era

Between 1642 and 1660, a period of political turmoil and civil war ravaged the kingdom of Great Britain. The Puritans rose against the king's power and searched for support in the most conservative sectors of the Parliament. King Charles I from the Stuart family of Scotland had attempted to re-establish Catholicism in the country, provoking a strong reaction among the Protestant subjects. He was accused of treason and beheaded. Oliver Cromwell seized power and established a republic in 1649 (Encyclopaedia Britannica, 2023b). During this period, theaters were shut down.

English society reached high levels of violence during the years of the civil war. Republicans embraced Puritanism and wanted to reinforce the Parliament to limit the power of the king. At the same time, royalists from England, Scotland, and Ireland searched for the restoration of absolute monarchy.

On May 25th, 1660, the civil war and the Puritan period ended when Charles II landed in York. He was the son of King Charles I and was there to claim the throne. He took advantage of the weak legitimacy of George Cromwell, who was the ruler at the moment. Charles II seized power and took revenge for his father's execution. He ordered to exhume Cromwell's body where it was hung, beheaded, and later, publicly exposed. Despite his bloody entrance, that was the only revengeful action Charles II took. He pardoned all the people involved in the revolution (Royal Museums Greenwich, n.d.).

Charles II abolished the laws Cromwell and the Parliament passed during the republic, including the lockdown of theaters. Theatrical activity flourished again. Theaters reopened, and playwrights' works were performed once more. There were so many new plays on stage that the period became a landmark in theater's history in Great Britain, known as the Restoration Theater (Cartwright, 2022).

The Impact of the English Civil War on Theater

Before the revolution, many conservatives, including Puritans, considered theater more than just entertainment. It was the expression of political opinions and the exposure of the good and evil in society. They felt the theater was a source of sinful and immoral thoughts and behaviors that they perceived as a threat to order and stability.

However, some Puritans weren't against theaters per se. In fact, they supported and even became patrons of theatrical companies that questioned the absolute power of the monarchs (Bawcutt, 2009). As explained, during the Elizabethan era, theater flourished, even being used to challenge the monarchs.

When the revolution and the civil war unfolded,

theaters were closed, but not to shut down opposing voices that might have benefited the revolutionary cause. Instead, theaters were closed as a security measure. The government was more concerned about social unrest and the increase in the levels of violence in the streets than the spread of specific ideas (Bawcutt, 2009).

The Parliament passed the first law that banned theatrical activities in September 1642, at the beginning of the conflict. However, the reasons for keeping them closed changed as the civil war evolved. At first, the most significant concern was a military invasion of Irish forces that wanted to re-establish the Stuart dynasty in power. Therefore, all the coastal places became potential targets for a foreign attack. In London, most theaters—especially the most popular—were located near the Thames River, a high-risk area.

Later, after the outbreak of the civil war, London was engulfed in a political crisis inside Parliament, and on the streets, Puritan-Republicans confronted royalists. Theaters were closed to prevent this confrontation from triggering open armed conflicts in public and the theaters. In 1647, a new law added the persecution of offenders to the current prohibition of theatrical presentations, giving the local governments the power to arrest the actors (Crowley, 2019).

Theaters remained closed for 18 years. Regardless of the reasons, it caused significant hardships for all the people involved in theatrical companies: theater owners, the companies' managers, playwrights, and the actors. The consequences were dramatic. Since no plays were presented on stage and therefore had no revenue, many theaters were abandoned and turned into ruins. Others were demolished.

Despite this hostile environment, the theater didn't

disappear. They resisted by moving underground. They worked outside the law, presenting short plays called 'drolls' in taverns, as they had done in the past. They promoted plays by distributing pamphlets in the streets (Crowley, 2019). Other companies and troupes performed at private houses. Nonetheless, the thriving theater developed through the Elizabethan era was paused.

Restoration Theater

The Restoration period started when Charles II seized power in 1660. The new king was a theater sympathizer. He spent his early years in a court where masques and theater were frequent. These spectacles made a great impression on young Charles. When he became king, he allowed theatrical presentations to flourish again.

The theaters reopened after almost 20 years of inactivity. However, Charles only allowed two companies to perform: the King's Company and the Duke's Company, with the writers Thomas Killigrew and William Davenant. The latter had produced *The Siege of Rhodes* at his house in 1656, even though theaters were still prohibited. That play is considered the first English opera.

The two companies benefited from the king's favor and held a virtual monopoly on theatrical activity in London. This monopoly endured until the 19th century. Davenant opened the Royal Theater at Covent Garden (Gainsborough, 2011). Later, the Duke's Company, led by Davenant, owned the Dorset Garden Theatre, also known as Duke of York's Theatre. It was designed by Sir Cristopher Wren, the famous architect of St. Paul's Cathedral. It became the most important theater in London and cost about £9,000 (750 thousand dollars today) to be built (V&A, n.d.). Killigrew opened The Royal Theater in Drury Lane. It became the first theater of the West End (Google Arts & Culture, n.d.).

The new theaters' structures differed from those built in the Elizabethan era. The new theaters each had a proscenium arch. This arch framed the stage and separated it from the audience with a curtain that closed and opened when the play started. There was a space between the proscenium arch and the place on stage where the performers deployed the acts. That created a sense of depth from the perspective of the audience.

The new theaters were prepared for more complex productions, including several acts, and actors and actresses had to come up and down the stage to change clothes. The stages had at least three doors, all placed behind the arch. Therefore, whenever costume changes or scenography were needed, the curtain closed, and the spectators couldn't see behind the scenes. Nonetheless, plays had a structure that marked the moments when the curtain closed and opened. The changes between one act and another were usually accompanied by music.

The building and maintenance of the theaters grew costlier, along with the productions. Therefore, ticket prices soon became more expensive (Gainsborough, 2011). Nonetheless, theater was a business, and companies looked forward to selling as many tickets as possible. The most expensive tickets were the best located, mainly close to the stage, or isolated boxes on the balconies on the first floor. On the side, the cheapest tickets were those in the two side galleries.

By 1700, the new theaters of the Restoration had a capacity of 650 seats. It is a significantly high number for a city of about 575,000 people (Demographia, n.d.).

Londoners of all social classes and tastes were avid theatergoers.

Restoration theater didn't offer deep plays on human beings' spirits or transcendental historical characters and events. Still, they brought innovation in the visual quality of presentations. The new theaters were enclosed buildings, not open venues, as most were in the Elizabethan era. They used artificial light, mainly provided by chandeliers hanging from the roof. This enabled them to present plays at night and not depend on sunlight to allow the audience to view their presentations.

The enclosed environment allowed the performers and playwrights to play with their imaginations. They could recreate any moment of the day or weather conditions. To achieve that, the companies added all types of special effects, including painting the stages and walls surrounding them. Theatrical productions continued to be more elaborate as time passed by.

Exploration of Societal Norms and Conventions—The Restoration Theater Genres

Restoration theater wasn't only about buildings and facilities. The content of the plays also changed. The Restoration period was filled with operas and dramatic plays, mainly comedies, the favorite genre acclaimed by the audiences. The social and political context had changed after the civil war, and so had the entertainment objectives. Restoration theater was much more commercial than Elizabethan theater. Restoration theater didn't pursue any educational or political purpose. Instead, it was immoral: "The dramatists did not criticize the accepted morality about gambling, drink, love, and pleasure generally, or try, like the dramatists of our own time, to work out their own view of character and conduct" (Crowley, 2019, para. 5).

The climate of the new court greatly influenced the content of the plays. Charles II was famous for the "cosmopolitan, libertine character of his court [...] where (...), 'anything went, where actresses were regularly rogered, where whores were ennobled to duchesses, where the arts flourished, where if greed wasn't yet good, hypocrisy certainly was'" (Oxford History of Western Music, n.d.). That framed the development of theater under his patronage, and he used it to gain popular support.

This period under Charles' rule was known as the Caroline era.

Operas and semi-operas were the most popular genres. They were based on Shakespeare's plays and those of other Renaissance playwrights. They combined music, dancing, singing, performing, and innovative special effects. Classical plays were adapted to popular taste. For instance, Shakespeare's *Macbeth* had witches dancing on stage (Gainsborough, 2011).

Almost every play incorporated music into the plays between the acts, while scenography and songs were prepared for the following action scene. This is now called 'incidental music.' Incidental music enabled cooperation between playwrights and composers in creating this new type of play. The music consisted of an overture that followed the French style Charles brought from exile. These overtures contained dances, songs, and instrumental music accompanying the performers' actions (Oxford History of Western Music, n.d.).

Charles II also promoted the presentation of masques, which was very frequent in the Stuart court before the revolution. The Restoration masques were a more polished version of the Jacobean ones. Dance and songs were alternated with dialogue and well-defined plots. A celebrated masque was *The Empress of Morocco*, composed by Matthew Locke in collaboration with the writers Thomas Shadwell and Thomas Betterton. The story about the Greek mythological characters Orpheus and Eurydice was a masque but with the new features of the opera. This play, performed at the Dorset Garden Theater by the Duke's Company, is considered the first 'dramatick opera' (Oxford History of Western Music, n.d.).

The music, the sound, and the visual effects of the new plays made clear that the primary purpose of theater was entertainment. Plays were adapted to the taste of the frivolous high class but also that of theatergoers of all social classes. The preferred genre was comedy.

Restoration comedy developed different sub-genres: the farce, the satire, the comedy of manners, and comedies of provincial humor. The plots revolved around love stories and intriguing affairs, questioning marriage as dull and depicting the rivalry between the sexes. The characters and the situations were stereotypically portrayed (men versus women, the good against the bad, and so on) and mainly represented the urban upper class. The stories were grotesquely presented, with several gross allusions to adultery and sexual attraction.

The comedy of manners was the most popular. It was called that way because it represented a mockery of the aristocracy's moral values and customs. The main characters were the stereotypical inhabitants of London: the countryman, the gentleman, and the Puritan, among others. Each of them is deliberately characterized by some particular feature. For instance, the Puritan was portrayed as a hypocrite, and the countryman was rude. While theater didn't have a political purpose, it did reflect the changes of the time. Puritanism and the past period were ridiculed, and, therefore, the new royalty was flattered. For people, it meant the end of the restrictive Puritan morality.

Leading Actresses and Their Celebrated Performances

Among the many changes in the Caroline period, perhaps the most significant was the allowance of women to perform female roles. Women could become professional actresses and playwrights for the first time. Margaret Huges is credited for being the first woman to perform as a professional actress in England. She played Desdemona in Shakespeare's *Othello*, presented in the Vere Street Theatre in 1660. Nell Gwyn, Elizabeth Barry, and Sarah Siddons, the "queen of tragedy," were some of the most famous actresses in the Restoration period.

Also, women became professional playwrights and were paid for their jobs. A famous group of writers called 'The Female Wits' produced several plays between the last decades of the 17th century and the beginning of the 18th century. Mary Pix, Susannah Cenrlivre, and Catharine Trotter were former members of that group. Aphra Behn was another prolific playwright of that time.

Even though women were admitted as professionals in the theater business, their immediate impact was limited by their gender. The presence of women on stage caught the morbid attention of the audience. The climate of the times, shaped by the lowering of morality and the content of the plays, left women in the role of sensual objects. Instead of becoming opposing characters that confronted or contrasted with the men, women were mere sexual accessories.

A typical scene reserved for women was the 'couch scene,' where a half-naked woman lay on a couch in the middle of the stage, acting to be asleep. Other plays went further and included a 'rape scene' (Sartika, 2016). The purpose wasn't to depict the violence against women but to exacerbate morbidity. Women were also assigned male characters, so they had to wear stretched breeches, exposing the shape of the female legs. That was considered highly erotic for 17th-century people. There was a long path ahead before women were respected in the arts for their talent, not their bodies.

The Impact of Prominent Theater Companies and Their Stars

Restoration theater was under a virtual monopoly controlled by the two companies allowed by the king: The Duke's Men and The King's Company. They were owned and directed by a manager who also was the leading actor. The plays were written and arranged to allow them to expose their abilities and talents.

In the Elizabethan era, companies had a horizontal organization and shared revenue. Restoration companies were somewhat different. The rest of the crew was hired for a particular play or a period and were paid a certain amount. The managers didn't share the income in equal parts but also didn't share the losses if the play wasn't successful.

The actors' salaries depended on several factors. They were specially trained to perform specific roles (the villain, the swordsman, and so on), and the wages were higher as the role was more complex or more important. Actors and actresses also received different payments depending on their popularity (Sartika, 2016). Just like Hollywood stars in the present, renowned actors were more likely to attract the audience and, therefore, had a higher *cachet*. Most became professionals through years of work on the stage instead of taking acting lessons.

Theater performers became more popular and achieved a status similar to nobility in London. They became celebrities and had their own troupes of fans. David Garrick was one of the most popular actors of the Restoration theater. He excelled using his natural style of acting, while most of the actors had overacted mannerisms. He became the Royal Theater's leading actor in 1741 and developed a sparkling career for over 30 years. One of Garrick's most celebrated performances was as King Lear, Shakespeare's tragedy.

As the leading actor, he was also a manager of the Drury Lane Theater. He implemented a series of changes, including constant rehearsals of the actors, not only before starting the season. He was also a playwright with over 20 plays written, including adaptations of Shakespeare's plays. He became the most famous actor of his time in Great Britain.

Chapter 4
The Rise of West End

West End refers to the west side of London's city center. It is located north of the Thames River and surrounded by the famous Camden and Westminster. In the 18th century, Westminster was, in fact, another city within the administration of London. It used to be referred to as "the Town" but has since adopted the name West End. "The Town" was composed of St. James's Palace, St. James's Square, Oxford and Bond Streets, and Piccadilly.

During the Middle Ages, this place had been home to the poor who tried to survive on the city's outskirts. Later, during the 17th and 18th centuries, the area became particularly famous, especially for the upper class. It was a privileged location in the city as the wind would blow away the smoke that came from the center of London (West End, 2019). The nobility established their residences there. Thus, the West End was home to many palaces and mansions, including the Palace of Westminster, where Parliament functions today.

The turning point for the city's spread to the West was

after the Great Fire of London. In 1666, a fire started in a bakery in Pudding Lane near London Bridge, near the river. By then, most houses in London were made of wood and the roofs out of straw. This enabled the fast propagation of the flames that destroyed major parts of the city, including Saint Paul's Cathedral. After the fire, the city was rebuilt, but this time, it went over its medieval boundaries and spread to the West End. It became the favorite place for nobility to settle and soon became the capital's most elegant and flourishing area.

The Influence of Urban Expansion and Population Growth

The first demographic distribution changes in London were created by royalty after the Glorious Revolution of 1688 (Vickery & Greig, 2022). The changes in the culture and dynamics of the city were led not by a plebeian bourgeoisie but by a liberal political class that transformed and modernized London. The new political regime played a key role in developing the West End, establishing a regular annual parliament that concentrated the aristocracy in the area.

The area where the elite lived soon became a pole of commerce for fashionable goods. The West End became the center of the evolution of commercial activity in London, encouraging more aristocracy to visit. The square where the wealthy concentrated was small enough to cover it by foot. People circulated there, from Parliament to the court, and shopped in the streets. Consumers soon boosted businesses in the area and outlined a type of consumption habits.

At this moment in the 18th century, there wasn't one point that concentrated all political activity or a single palace where all the royalty affairs took place. Therefore, the aristocracy's public and cultural life was relatively dispersed (Vickery & Greig, 2022). People were in permanent motion during the season of parliamentary business, between October and May. The active life in the city led to early concrete paving and illumination of the streets of West End.

Another significant economic and social process unfolded in the late 18th century in Great Britain that contributed to the shaping of the West End. The Industrial Revolution meant deep and massive changes in society. The phenomenon rapidly spread to most of the Western European countries, but it exploded in England. The emergence of factories and the intensification of commerce made Great Britain the first society of consumption. Massive migrations from the countryside to the cities made the city of London flourish and develop at a dramatic pace.

The new economic system shaped a new society. The production to cover primary needs was replaced by a need to earn and have money not only to survive but to buy things—things that are needed and those that are wanted. The key to the changes in consuming habits was the new middle working class and the reinforcement of the industrial-commercial bourgeoisie (West End Universe, 2023).

London had already consolidated as the biggest city in Europe and the most important port. It was the greatest producer of silver and golden goods and many other manufactured items, even before the Industrial Revolution. While the working and lower classes settled in the East of the city, the aristocracy and the upper class concentrated in the West End.

The Growth of the West End as a Theater District

As society changed, the city and the public spaces evolved to keep pace with the new rhythm. Shops, stores, and public office buildings became concentrated in the West, as did cultural activities. During the second half of the 17th century, theaters regained the glory of the times before the revolution and moved to where the city's life flourished: The West End.

The first theater in the West End was Drury Lane Theater. It belonged to Thomas Killigrew, a theater manager; later, it was managed by his successor, Colley Cibber. The original building burned down during the Fire of London but reopened in Covent Garden in 1674. The new building, designed by Sir Cristopher Wren, is the oldest theater in London that continues to be active even at present.

The Restoration era boosted the emergence of more theaters across London. The companies increased their revenue, and managers had the resources to invest. One of them, John Rich from the Duke's Company, wanted to have a big theater of his own to compete with Drury Lane, but he had to wait a long time before he finally had the financial backup.

Rich had inherited the Lincoln's Inn Fields Theatre from his father, and in 1728, his luck was about to change. The producer, John Gay, presented a blockbuster—*The Beggar's Opera*—with a record of 62 performances (Britannica Encyclopaedia, 2022). It was a great success at the time, and Rich finally had what he needed to have his theater in the West End.

In 1732, Rich opened his own theater in the West End:

the Convent Garden Theater. It was located where the Royal Opera House stands in modern times. It was the most prominent and fanciest theater in London, with seats for 1,000 spectators at the time of opening, and increased to 3,000 in the following years. The accommodations had boxes for the higher classes, the galleries, and the pit with the lowest prices. Rich presented the comedy *The Way of the World* by William Congreve for the opening show.

The Restoration era motivated many producers and managers to open theaters, and they saw the growing audiences. Many theaters, such as the Little Theater and Sadler's Wells, opened beyond the West End and even in the provinces (Dickson, 2018). Theatrical companies developed, presenting more and better produced shows as Londoners became more enthusiastic about theater.

However, the authorities decided to increase control of the theatrical shows and passed the Licensing Act in 1737. By this point, theatrical activity was already restricted by the monopoly given to the main companies. The Licensing Act established a new stage of censorship on drama plays. It stated that any play should be reviewed and approved by Lord Chamberlain and the Examiners of Plays.

The Licensing Act was passed by the Prime Minister Robert Walpole. Lord Chamberlain was assigned full power to censor or prohibit plays from being performed if they had some type of subversive content.

The act deeply impacted the evolution of theater in Great Britain. The opening of new theaters didn't stop, but managers preferred producing and presenting classical plays, especially those by Shakespeare, instead of new plays that could fall under the law. Playwrights' importance and social status decreased. It also caused theatrical activity to be concentrated outside London, where censorship didn't reach so intensely (Thomas, 2014).

At the beginning of the 19th century, there was a new shift in the course of the West End's history. The playwright John Scott invested £10,000 to build the first major theater in the West End despite the remaining constraint of the Licensing Act. It was called the Sans Pareil (the Adelphi Theater at the present day) (West End, 2019).

A new age of flourishing started in the middle of the century. In 1843, new legislation ended the monopoly King Charles gave to The Duke and Lord Chamberlain companies. From then on, companies could present spoken drama plays in other playhouses beyond the Royal Theater and the Covent Garden.

By the 1850s, many immigrants came from the continent to England after the failed revolution of 1848. They spent their savings on buildings that were perfect to serve as theaters. Until the 1860s, theater wasn't the most profitable business because the working class didn't attend drama plays massively. However, that began to change in the 1860s, and from then on, dozens of theaters were built in London. Most of those new theaters were located in the West End. The changes that continued to set a landmark in the West End history are framed in what was known as the Victorian era.

In the second half of the century, the authorities couldn't hold the Licensing Act any longer since people clamored for and requested the comeback of theatrical plays. When the act was dropped in 1843, several theaters opened: the Vaudeville Theater and the Savoy Theater, both in the Strand, and the Criterion at Piccadilly Circus. The Savoy opened to present Gilbert and Sullivan's comedies and operas. It was the first theater lit entirely with electric lights (Jaramillo & Guichard, 2020).

The Emergence of English-Language Musicals

The restrictive legal frame imposed by the Restoration government hampered the development of dramatic presentations. The monopoly and the Licensing Act discouraged play producers and playwrights from taking plays on stage and led them to operate outside this frame. In this context, a new genre flourished: musicals. The monopoly only allowed the two main companies to present theatrical plays but didn't say anything about musical shows. So, theater managers presented musical entertainment in new, smaller theaters and music halls.

Music was the key.

During the 19th century, small music halls were opened across London, outside the West End and the capital. There was a special license to perform a few "burlettas." These are plays of three acts with at least five musical numbers. The burlettas were specially produced to be performed at minor theaters and emerged as a way to avoid legal restrictions (Stars of the Edwardian Stage, n.d.).

While some theaters presented silent shows, others developed genres where music accompanied the actions. Since there were no words or poetry, the spectacles needed to add more resources to make it more attractive to the audience. Therefore, they included more scenographic resources, visual effects, and performing arts such as acrobatics, magic, and comedy sketches.

Meanwhile, the theater returned to where it had started a couple of centuries ago: taverns and coffeehouses that turned into music halls, mainly in the East End, where the lower classes lived and gathered. There, musical shows were presented while people ate and drank. They were usually played by amateur artists, and they played light music on Saturday afternoons to amuse the audience, mainly composed of the working class. These shows became more popular, and soon, music hall rooms opened to receive the middle class in the 1830s.

One of the first places that served as a music hall was the Eagle. It was at City Road and Shepherdess Walk in the East End. It became particularly trendy in 1854. Marie Lloyd premiered there at the age of 14, barely older than a child, and became one of the big stars of music halls. The place was later demolished, but, at present, a pub is open at the same location, and visitors and locals alike can go there to listen to old music pieces from earlier times.

Taverns and coffee shops allowed working-class women to attend performances, something that was prohibited in supper rooms. Women would even bring their children to the shows. Therefore, these places were a way to democratize access to these cultural events, which later impacted the content of the plays. Companies and playwrights saw the potential of family audiences and added family-friendly elements to the plays.

As music halls gained a reputation, managers began to invest in buildings with the specific purpose of presenting these shows. The first of them was the Canterbury Hall in Lambeth. It belonged to Charles Morton and opened in 1852. It had a capacity for 700 people who didn't only listen to music but also had tables to eat and drink. The tickets were very accessible, so the middle and lower classes could afford to attend the shows.

The actor and singer Sam Cowell became a success at

Canterbury. His very name grew such a convening power that the manager needed to build a larger room. The new building could host over 1,500 people and had two ticket prices, depending on the seating location, to enjoy the performance. The room had balconies with an art gallery and was decorated with chandeliers. These comfortable accommodations allowed the best view of the show and, therefore, the tickets were more expensive. Everyone else sat in the lower galleries with much more affordable tickets.

Due to Morton's success, many music hall rooms opened in London. By 1875, there were about 300 music halls across the city, which meant more workplaces for performers, singers, musicians, and composers. The entertainment industry expanded thanks to the increasing popularity of music halls. They became a place for social promotion and also to introduce women to other spaces of society. Women were welcomed in music hall performances. For them, it was a way to earn a living, have social appreciation, and escape from the time's limitations.

These shows were performed at the Sans Pareil Theater in the West End, which opened in 1806. At present, that is the Adelphi Theater. Burlesque and melodrama were also popular genres, and the comic operas were written by Gilbert and Sullivan. During the 1870s and 1880s, musical theater had over 500 performances. Gilbert and Sullivan presented over a dozen of opera comedies. *H.M.S. Pinafore* and *The Mikado* were the company's longest-running shows. *The Chimes of Normandy* and *Dorothy* were the most enduring plays on stage, with over 700 and 900 performances, respectively.

Actors also developed a new style of performance based on movements and gestures, usually accompanied by music. They had to keep the attention of an active crowd that

How the West End Became the West End

searched to be involved in the presentation from the moment they arrived. Sarah Siddons, Edmund Kean, Henry Irving, and T.P. Cooke were some of the new stars of the London stages. The latter represented Frankenstein for the first time. Some of those names are closely associated with the Victorian era, which we will cover in the following section.

By the end of the century, theater managers improved musicals, adding family-friendly content, professional dancers, and popular songs. Then, musicals consolidated as a different genre within the theater. The manager, George Edwardes, wanted to provide a better quality show that was different from the old burlesque, and it turned into a new musical genre: the Edwardian musical comedy. It developed under the rule of King Edward VII, but it prevailed until the beginning of World War I.

Edwardian musical comedy was characterized by its simple plots. The content was family-friendly, and the plays had attractive fashion and costume displays. By then, theater plays included exciting new technology, such as electric lights, to create special effects on stage.

Manager Edwards bought the Gaiety Theater when Gilbert and Sullivan's opera dominance had ended. Edwardes, also called "'he Guv'nor," added a dancing corp composed of girls to the plays. Among his most famous plays, we can name *The Shop Girl* (1894) and *A Runaway Girl* (1898). Soon, all the theaters of London brought this type of musical to their stages, and it was copied even in other places in Europe and America. It was the beginning of musicals, and the style would be predominant for the following decades.

Chapter 5

Victorian Splendor

In the 17th century, Queen Elizabeth's reign was a landmark for Great Britain and London theater. In the 19th century, another woman came to the throne to revolutionize not only the political life of the kingdom but also lead a stream of changes that would give her name to a new era. She was Queen Victoria.

The name of the era isn't limited to the 64 years of her reign but represents the period of British history that goes between 1820 and 1914, before the outbreak of World War I. Nonetheless, the name of Victoria credits the queen for her leadership that turned Great Britain into the most powerful nation in the world.

She was the last monarch of the House of Hannover and the first one of the House of Windsor, who still rule the United Kingdom at the present. She reached the throne while very young, at only 18 years old. Nonetheless, she introduced revolutionary measures such as allowing all people to vote and abolishing slavery in all the British imperial possessions. Her name was associated with times of stability, wealth, and a flourishing culture.

During this era, theater experienced a new period of splendor. The entertainment industry had grown, despite the Licensing Act, by the emergence of music halls. After the government loosened the legal restrictions on drama, theaters opened throughout London. After 1843, the number of playhouses increased, as did the city's population and the working class's spending power. The sprawling audiences turned the theater into a profitable and attractive business for a consolidated bourgeoisie willing to invest.

This became the time that large companies took their plays on tours, and flashy actors and managers' names took the spotlight. During the Victorian era, opera became one of the audience's favorite genres. While music halls and variety shows continued to be popular, new audiences—mainly from the middle and lower classes—wanted more realistic stories and characters that reflected their lives. Therefore, melodrama and pictorial drama evolved—the content of the plays became important again.

The Dominance of Melodrama in Victorian Theater

During the previous period, the topics presented on stage were less important than the visual features of presentations. Pre-Victorian era shows displayed music, colorful dresses, and easy entertainment over intense dialogues and heavy-hearted scripts. Theater during the Victorian era was very different from this. Famous playwrights who covered current topics took their works to the stage to entertain and give theater back its social and political role of educating and shaping opinions, especially for the working class, which was then the largest audience.

The Victorian era was framed by the rise of the bourgeoisie and the emergence of revolutionary movements in Europe, such as socialism and communism. The workers found in these ideals a way to express discontent with their social conditions and fight against oppression. It was also a time when women gained new spaces in society. They had access to culture and to positions in the work market which had been previously unreachable. All those aspects of society needed to be expressed somewhere, and the theaters' stages were one such place.

Theater during the Victorian era was in a transition between Romanticism and Neoclassicism. The first appealed to emotions, and the main purpose was to move the audience. Neoclassicism, though, put the actors in the center of the scene. In addition, Victorian theater was characterized by a high level of social commentary. It wasn't only about pursuing beauty but reflecting the world the people were living in.

The typical genre of Victorian theater was melodrama. The first melodrama in Great Britain is credited to Thomas Holcroft, who presented *A Tale of Mystery* in 1802. Melodramas consisted of short acts and musical presentations. Stories revolved around simple stereotypical characters, and the most common issues were related to moral values. The villain, the heroine, the hero, and the triumph of good over evil were typical Victorian plays.

Simple stories were displayed with intense performances by the actors on stage. The sentimental plots often tell the story of improbable adversities that the characters had to face before finally reaching a happy end. The suffering maiden and her hero had to struggle against the villain through a sequence of spectacular scenes where virtues and flaws were overcome, and the moments of great tension were accompanied by music to intensify the moment.

By the middle of the 19th century, another space for entertainment opened. This time, it was specially targeted at women. During the Victorian era, a new habit was adopted by the citizens. Due to industrialization, the evening meal was eaten later. Therefore, a new meal was added in the afternoon: tea and pastries. Soon, tea rooms opened in London, and this habit became a social movement for gathering for women.

There, women had the opportunity to spend time with other women, share their thoughts, and discuss ideas without the company of their husbands. It was an early expression of feminism. Music was performed at those tea rooms, and tearjerkers appeared. Musicians and, sometimes, brief theatrical presentations were performed as the ladies enjoyed their afternoon tea. All the performances embodied the characteristics of the melodramas: They were intended to move the audience.

These tea rooms were also places where women could start a career as singers and performers. Marie Lloyd, Vesta Tilley, and Gertie Millar are some of the women with a working-class background who began performing as music hall artists in tea rooms and became stars in the country. While this was a space of opportunities for women, it also contributed to enclosing them in gender-associated roles within the entertainment industry.

Charles Kean and Samuel Phelps' Performances

Even though William Shakespeare was a successful playwright in the Elizabethan era and his plays continued to be presented on stage, it was during the 19th century when his work became an icon of British culture. Victorian intellectuals and artists weren't interested in Shakespeare for his talent and the artistic value of his work but for the political and moral messages that could be taken from his plays.

The devotion to Shakespeare during the Victorian era manifested in different events to honor the writer: museum and painting exhibitions; celebrations at the places where he had been; banquets and speeches to refer to his greatness; monuments and statues of the playwright. His most famous plays were performed in all the theaters of London. Shakespeare's style and tragedies perfectly depicted Victorian society and the place theater had within it.

The performers created the dramatic effect through their voices, the way they pronounced their lines, and their gestures rather than by the surrounding effects. It wasn't only the lines written by Shakespeare but how they were pronounced and recited by the performers. Two names stand out among the actors during the Victorian era: Charles Kean and Samuel Phelps. They built their reputation performing the most relevant characters depicted by Shakespeare.

Charles Kean was the son of the popular actor Edmund Kean, who had belonged to the Drury Lane company. Charles debuted in 1827 in London with the play *Douglas*, which also toured in the United States. He rose to stardom with a celebrated performance of *Hamlet* and *Richard III*. Although he didn't only perform Shakespeare's main characters' roles, it was those roles that made him a name among theatrical performers.

Kean's performance of *Hamlet* at Covent Garden in 1838 caught the attention of Queen Victoria. Some years later, the queen hired him to run private theatrical entertainments at Windsor Castle. Later, Kean also became the manager of the Princess's Theater, where he produced several Shakespeare revivals. *A Midsummer Night's Dream* was the audience's favorite play (National Portrait Gallery, n.d.).

Charles Kean was often presented as a rival of Samuel Phelps, the other leading player of this time. Phelps had his debut at the Haymarket Theater in 1837. He played Shylock in Shakespeare's *The Merchant of Venice*. After his short time at the Haymarket Theater, he spent six years at Covent Garden and performed at Drury Lane. Besides starring in Shakespeare's plays, he performed in Sir Walter Scott's novels, such as *The Fortunes of Nigel* and *Ivanhoe*. His last appearance on stage personified Cardinal Wolsey in the play *Henry VIII* by Shakespeare.

Besides being a famous actor, Phelps was also a renowned and successful theater manager. He was the Sadler's Wells Theatre's manager in association with Thomas L. Greenwood and Mary Amelia Warner for 20 years. During all those years, Phelps presented 34 plays written by Shakespeare, reflecting the fascination of Victorian society for his work.

Theatrical Adaptations of Dickens' Novels

Besides theater, literature also flourished during the Victorian era. Names like Sir Walter Scott, Jane Austen, and the Brontë sisters soon became household staples. Among those names, Charles Dickens emerged as one of the symbols of Victorian literature. Despite mainly writing novels and a few less-known plays, Dickens was closely related to Victorian theater. He was an enthusiastic theatergoer and an actor himself. Even though he didn't reach the most prominent theatrical companies, he performed several times in front of Queen Victoria and her husband.

While Dickens's plays didn't meet with much success, his novels were adapted to the stage almost immediately after being published. Those plays were so successful that his stories were performed even in the printing stage, sometimes even before they were completed (Davis, n.d.).

One of the keys to Dickens's success on stage was that the audience was already familiar with the stories because they had read the novels first. This built new connections between theatrical presentations and other cultural products, as once happened with music.

Dickens's work in the Victorian era is some of the most essential literature in history due to the content he covered in his books. Some of his most famous novels, such as *Oliver Twist, A Tale of Two Cities,* and *A Christmas Carol*, depicted Victorian society in all its harshness. He covered issues like poverty, exclusion, and workers' living conditions. The lower classes were humanized and were given faces and names. Moreover, Dickens was the only successful author writing about the poor. While the other writers spoke mainly about the wealthy classes, all of Dickens's characters were workers or the deprived. Dickens broke the barriers of the idea that only the upper classes were worth writing about. The stories and the characters were relatable to many audience members, and the readers felt empathy for them. Dickens's work helped Victorian society become aware of the contradictions of progress and industrialization.

Dickens's stories condensed all the elements of Victorian narrative and, therefore, worked well on Victorian theater stages. The plays had all the elements of melodrama: "'the curtain lines, the emotional exchanges, the direct appeals to those beyond the footlights" (Ferguson, 2001, p. 732). His stories helped shape Victorian society and promote changes.

Oscar Wilde's Plays

As the century progressed, people's interest in current social affairs grew, and theatrical companies doubled their efforts to present more realistic plays. Oscar Wilde was one of the most prominent playwrights of the West End during the Victorian era. In the present day, he is better remembered as the author of the novel *The Picture of Dorian Grey*.

While Dickens focused on depicting social inequalities and described the hardships of the lower classes, Wilde dedicated himself to delving into human nature regardless of social position. Moreover, he exposed his times' double morality and hypocrisy by satirizing social expectations and conventional roles. His first famous plays were *Lady Windermere's Fan* (1892) and *An Ideal Husband* (1895). The first play premiered at the St James's Theatre in 1892, and the other at the Haymarket Theatre in 1895. They were both blockbusters.

Also, in 1895, Wilde presented perhaps his most remembered play: *The Importance of Being Earnest*. It was a comedy that criticized marriage and the social obligations of Victorian society. It was his last play since he was involved in a series of legal matters that accused him of sodomy—having a sexual relationship with another man. He was eventually found guilty and arrested.

Wilde was released in 1897, but his reputation was already harmed by then. He had to move to France, where he wrote *Salome*, based on the biblical character. The play was forbidden in Great Britain by the Lord Chamberlain and wasn't produced until 1931, 30 years after Wilde's death.

Oscar Wilde was a symbol of Victorian spectacular theater since his plays perfectly depicted that era's theme of reproducing real life on stage using all types of visual effects and costumes. Besides this, he also became a symbol of the adversities that women and homosexuals faced during the Victorian era (Offord, 2017).

The Construction of Grand Victorian Theaters

During the 19th century, as the entertainment business grew, more theaters were built for the specific purpose of presenting musical and theatrical shows. The technological advances allowed managers to equip theaters with several new features to create more realistic and detailed scenographies.

The most important theater of the time was the Adelphi. It was first built in 1806 as the Sans Pareil but was reformed and redecorated several times during the century. It got the name Adelphi when the Adams brothers took it over. It was a big theater and the preferred venue for melodramas. The first adaptation of Dickens' novel was presented in this theater.

The Royal Albert Saloon was distinguished from others because it had two stages, one facing the audience and the other pointing to an outdoor theater. Burlesque and vaudeville plays were performed there, as well as ballets and music concerts.

The Criterion Theater, built in 1874, didn't only have a stage and an auditorium for theatrical plays. Due to the role of theaters as a place for social gatherings, especially of those from the upper classes and the bourgeois, they also had dining rooms, restaurants, ballrooms, and concert halls.

Other theaters built in the previous period continued to be the preferred stages by patrons, producers, and actors: the Convent Garden, Drury Lane, and the Royal Haymarket. At the end of the century, more famous theaters opened and presented the crowning plays of the Victorian era: the Vaudeville Theater, the Savoy, and the Lyric Theater.

In the past, many theaters were originally buildings used for another purpose before being adapted to host an audience and stage. In the Victorian era, theater buildings became a specific architectural design. Architects were assigned to make existing theaters bigger and to create new ones. The auditoriums had a larger capacity and with grand, luxurious rooms. Theaters' locations reflected social class differences.

There were balconies, galleries, and cheaper locations—the so-called 'pit'—so the theatergoers would enjoy the performance regardless of the ticket price they could afford. Theaters were organized to segregate the social classes not only where they sat and saw the show but also which entrance they would use, what facilities were available to them, and where they would mingle. The rooms for the higher classes were decorated with carpets and rich hanging lights, and the galleries for the working class were much more modest.

The auditorium was dark, and the lights were directed to the stage, creating a more striking effect. The invention of gas lighting allowed the creation of these unique environments in theaters, adapted to the requirements of the melodramas. Gas lighting was first implemented on stage in 1803 in the Lyceum Theater. Despite the cost, theater managers saw the possibilities to improve their presentations. The rows of lights were placed at different positions on the stage to create different effects. Later, engineers added a control valve that could regulate light intensity, and it was used according to the moments of the story.

Another significant invention was the limelight, which was incorporated into theaters in the 1840s. It was a direct point emitted by a cylindrical block and lit a sharp spot on the stage. It was used to follow and light the leading actors. It also created special effects such as moonlight, daylight, or even streaming waters.

Gas lighting was hazardous because it could cause a fire at any moment. By the end of the century, it would be replaced by electric lightning. In 1890, the incandescent mantle, which provided a whiter and brighter light, was invented. Even though the quality of the light improved, the risks of fires didn't wholly disappear. Nonetheless, it was a frequently used resource to increase the realism of the performance.

Notable Actors and Actresses of the Era

In Victorian theater, what happened on stage was more important than the words behind the scenes. The role of actors and their ability to move the audience were far more significant than the literary talent of the playwrights. At this time, playwrights weren't well paid, so they didn't make great efforts to create innovative and original stories. Most plays taken to the stage were adaptations of older plays, mainly by Shakespeare, from Dickens's novels or poorly developed stories and characters. The performers added all the magic.

The primary purpose of the actors was to make the spectators experience a touching moment, even if that meant walking away from what was written in the script. Victorian actors were characterized by the improvised dialogues and movements they came up with as they were performing. This led them to create a unique style that hadn't been seen before, creating a new sense of excitement in the audience to know these talented actors. Theater actors and actresses became celebrities, and being theater stars provided them with high social recognition.

Leading actors owned their own companies or had enough influence to arrange plays where they could be the stars. It was usual that renowned actors passed down their place within the companies and on stage to their sons or that theater managers opened a theater to boost the acting careers of their sons and daughters.

One of those families, probably the most prominent, was the Kean's. Edmund Kean is considered by many to be the best tragic actor of his time. He performed Shylock in Shakespeare's *The Merchant of Venice* at Drury Lane Theater in 1814. Later, his son, Charles Keane, also became a prestigious actor renowned for his roles in Shakespearean tragedies. Edmund initially discouraged his son from a theatrical career but eventually included him in his plays. They were performing *Othello* in 1833 when Edmund died on stage.

Women also entered the acting business and significantly contributed to theater's development. Lucia Vestris was an actress and the manager of the Olympic Theater, and she was the first to assemble music, acting, and visual effects as one unit. She placed herself as the director of the plays and combined all the production elements. It was also her idea to build rooms behind or at the sides of the stage so the actors could enter without being seen by the audience.

Chapter 6
The Birth of Modern Drama

The first years of the 20th century before the outbreak of World War I are considered within the Victorian era. Performing arts deepened public interest in real life and current affairs. Since the last decades of the past century, the building of the theaters and the use of special effects have worked collaboratively to provide presentations with more realistic features.

By the end of the 19th century and the beginning of the 1900s, two new artistic movements consolidated and became the primary influence of theater in the West End: realism and naturalism.

Realism first developed in France in the middle of the 19th century and later reached Great Britain. It rejected the artificiality that characterized classicism and romanticism, which emphasized creating beauty and exacerbating shapes and colors to express emotions. Realism was an attempt to reproduce reality as the world is in actuality. The main topics covered by the realistic artists were the lives of everyday people, regarding their troubles and customs, and it aimed to reflect the structures of society.

Naturalism coincided with the evolution of scientism and positivism in the 19th century. Naturalism states that the main purpose of human beings is to know reality as it is through concrete evidence provided by nature. In the arts, it implied the attempt to depict reality "as it was." The main difference between both movements is that, while realism objectively describes reality from the outside, naturalism focuses on internal dialogues, and the narrator's voice almost disappears.

The Impact of Realism and Naturalism on Theater

The influence that these two movements had on the theater was evident during the 19th century. While they were two separate movements, we shall focus on the main elements that united both. Naturalism and realism focus on presenting stories in the most convincing and realistic possible way. There was an extra effort in providing details of the ordinary environments where the story took place, and the characters were carefully depicted not only through manners and words but also through the costumes and make-up. The storyline was simple so that the spectator could follow the moving story of each character.

Naturalistic plays followed the three main elements of drama (space, time, and action), and they used it to pair time on stage with real life. So, a two-hour play represented two hours in real-time. The story usually happened in a single place, and there weren't discontinuities between either place or time. Realistic plays used the 'box-set' structure. The stage represented the three walls of a room where the action occurred, and the fourth wall was imaginary on the side facing the audience.

The characters were often working-class people who were presented as victims of the determinants of their social and economic conditions. These plays also dared to cover taboo topics such as poverty, suicide, and prostitution. The drama is driven by psychological features like the characters' inner struggles and deep motivations. In realistic plays, the main character attempts to overcome the restrictions imposed by their environment and to thrive against the odds. The success of these genres can be explained by the way the spectators could identify themselves with the lives and struggles of the characters and find a little hope for achieving a more promising future.

The dialogue between the characters was written in the vernacular language that everyday people spoke. Poetic language, complex vocabulary, or extravagant pronunciation went against the realistic theater's goal of depicting relatable characters. Exaggerated movements and gestures were replaced with simple, ordinary manners, and the characters' stories displayed the tension and drama.

The Norwegian playwright Henrik Ibsen is considered the father of modern realism, and his most famous play, *A Doll's House*, is credited as the first play in history to use realism. It premiered on December 21st, 1879 in Copenhagen. The play argues against the social conventions of women's role in society. It tells the story of Nora, a woman who appears to live an idyllic life with a loving husband and their children. At the end of the play, she can't stand her husband's attitude towards her and leaves. She left her husband and children, which shook Victorian society and Europe (Cash, 2021).

The naturalistic theater was represented by the Russian playwright Anton Chekhov. His play *The Seagull* is considered a milestone in the evolution of naturalism in performing arts. Chekhov's plays were distinguished because they told stories where 'nothing happened.' His plays didn't have the traditional structure with a climax and a resolution; instead, he explored the drama of the undramatic. Chekhov attempted to present the world without moral judgment, and the characters didn't display any relevant action. Instead, ordinary events with no resolution were taken on stage (Lewis, n.d.a).

The Emergence of Independent Theater Movements

The evolution of realistic theater in the West End is associated with the emergence of the Independent Theater Society. This institution emerged in London as a side effect of the Licensing Act and censorship carried out by Lord Chamberlain. It started in 1891 and continued its activities until 1897.

The society was a by-subscription organization that would perform in theaters on Sundays when no public spectacles were scheduled. Since these presentations weren't open to the public but restricted to the members subscribed to the organization, the plays didn't need to be approved by The Lord Chamberlain. For example, professional actors performed two realistic and naturalistic theater plays by the society: *Ghosts* by Ibsen and *Thérèse Raquin* by the French novelist and playwright Émile Zola.

Independent theater could present plays that fell beyond the topics allowed by the law and also uncommercial plays. The earlier theaters, led by managers, clearly aimed to make money. Instead, independent theaters put the spotlight on the discussion of political ideas and criticizing social stereotypes, so they performed the plays the commercial theatrical companies rejected. Even though the authorities tried to ban these presentations, they could do little to prevent society from presenting controversial plays. However, their income wasn't enough to cover financial shortages, eventually leading to the organization's closure.

The Influence of the Irish Literary Theatre and Scottish Renaissance

The influences on the evolution of the West End theater weren't restricted to the artistic movements that reached Great Britain from the continent. During the 19th century, there was a strong mark of political uprising within the kingdom, coming from the nationalist vindications and revolutionary movements that started in Ireland.

The Irish people's desire to obtain independence from the British crown was reflected in a nationalistic cultural revival known as the Irish Literary Renaissance. It started with Standish James's *History of Ireland*, which was filled with mysticism and fantasy instead of realistic features. It attempted to revitalize the Gaelic ancestors of Ireland in opposition to British cultural supremacy.

This impulse led to the creation of the Gaelic League, founded by Douglas Hyde in 1893. He claimed the need to "de-anglicize" Ireland and called on the Irish to speak their original Gaelic. It was also the renaissance of Irish poetry and drama. Its evolution in the late 19th century dramatically differed from the realistic theater that became popular in the West End.

The most influential writer of this Irish movement was William Butler Yeats, a prominent representative of modernism in the early decades of the 20th century. His works mainly consisted of poetry with Irish nationalist vindications but were written in English. The topics revolved around Celtic myths and folklore—very distant from the typical issues depicted by realistic and naturalistic plays.

The Exploration of Political and Social Themes on Stage: George Bernard Shaw's Contributions

The first decades of the 20th century were very dramatic for the Western world. First, World War I had proved that liberalism wasn't enough to keep peace, and the crack of the Wall Street market in 1929 showed the weaknesses of capitalism. If realism and naturalism had helped visualize the unfortunate living conditions of the less fortunate, the Great Depression showed that no one was safe. The 19th century was a time of hope and blind trust in science and the power of human beings struggling to survive. The 20th century started as a time of deception and disappointment.

The new setting reached arts, understanding the critical position to expose reality in all its rawness. Social realism emerged in the 1930s with the Great Depression as the background. One of this theatrical movement's most prolific and renowned playwrights is the Irish playwright George Bernard Shaw.

His style contributed to shaping social realism in its attempt to depict a plain image of poverty, mainly of the forgotten rural population, usually excluded from all artistic expressions.

Shaw came to live in London and became an engaged socialist activist. He had a rough start in his professional career as a novelist. By the 1890s, he decided to become a playwright after the encouragement of an independent theater manager. By then, the London playwrights struggled to produce high-quality drama regarding the depth of the issues they were supposed to cover. Most plays of the time were light entertainment without any significant substance. This became more evident when Ibsen's plays were performed at the London West End. Shaw wanted to produce a play that could meet the style and excellence of Ibsen's plays, which were highly valued by the audience.

Shaw wrote his first play, *Widowers' Houses*, inspired by Ibsen's *A Doll's House*, to address controversial issues in his current society by turning naturalism into parody and satire. He soon developed his style of comedy (Lewis, n.d.b). He combined Ibsen's seriousness to treat controversial and uncomfortable issues and the tone of irony that Wilde used in his plays. Shaw attempted to use humor to expose the hypocrisy of the society of his time.

Poetic and Psychological Dramas

World War I plunged people into despair, and the arts displayed thoughts about humankind, the purpose of life, and the internal aspects of existence. The American writer Thomas Stearns Eliot is an example of how the environment reignited a style that had been discarded except by the Irish national theater and cultural movement. Eliot, who moved from America to England, revitalized British poetry and wrote essays that influenced literature and performing arts in the first decades of the 20th century.

Eliot established himself as a religious writer; he was a son of the Victorian era, and, as he said, he endeavored to describe the correspondence between the object that existed in real life and the words that named it (Davies et al., 2023).

Later, Eliot dedicated himself to writing plays targeted at an audience he believed was motivated by an unconscious pursuit of redemption in a world filled with grief. He used blank verses to write his plays and created popular drama to convey his message to the masses. His most famous plays are *Sweeney Agonistes, Murder in the Cathedral, The Family Reunion,* and *The Elder Statesman.* Some of them were modern versions of miracle plays. In contrast, others had a similar structure as ancient Greek plays, with a chorus and the exaltation of the hero figure.

The calamities unleashed by the war and the following economic crisis led people to avoid looking at reality as it was. Therefore, they searched for answers beyond reality. Eliot funneled that trend by reviving religious issues that appealed to people's faith.

August Strindberg, a Swedish writer, was another author who believed that people didn't want to see reality. Instead, they were more interested in the internal psychological processes that guided their actions and emotions. Strindberg's most famous plays are *The Father* and *Miss Julie*, in which he responded to Ibsen's works. Ibsen's plays were considered too feminist by the Swedish man. Instead, he tried to present the conflict between the sexes differently.

Strindberg was influenced by German Expressionism. Driven by Schopenhauer and Nietzsche's contributions, he migrated from the physical dimension to the realm of fantasy and magic. His later writings were plays about dreams, and they explored the human being's mind and spirit.

Like Ibsen's last stage of his career, Strindberg turned to the supernatural. It was taken on stage as a discontinuation of time and space, and the logical sequence of actions that characterized realism and naturalism was broken. Stridenberg wrote about his dream plays: "Anything can happen, everything is possible and plausible. Time and space do not exist. Upon an insignificant background of real-life events, the imagination spins and weaves new patterns: a blend of memories, experiences, pure inventions, absurdities, and improvisations" (Lewis, n.d.c, para. 3).

It was the prelude to a new cultural and artistic movement that started in philosophy and extended to all branches of art, including theater.

The Use of Symbolism and Non-Linear Narratives

Realism and naturalism had utilized an excess of resources to embellish reality in an attempt to depict it as it was. The 20th century witnessed the attempt of intellectuals and artists to interrupt the disturbing reality that surrounded them and create a new reality of their own. The new cultural movement that reflected that intention was called expressionism, and it proposed that objective reality didn't even exist. Instead, reality was a creation of the internal emotions of the subject.

Expressionist artists didn't pay attention to trivial ordinary situations but to general truths beyond them. These truths couldn't be represented like realistic scenes of the previous period since they are ideas. Therefore, expressionist theater returned to symbols to share their concept. The interest wasn't focused on the physical world but on the mental state of the individuals who couldn't be trapped in a specific time and place.

The stage and the scenography lost importance and became an accessory to dialogue. It became just the frame where the performers stood to pronounce extensive monologues. The attention was focused on words and the meaning of the lines. These generally revolved around the value of older generations and the morality of the bourgeoisie, as well as the possible revolutionary exits to their inherited problems. The narrative became non-linear, and instead of following a storyline, it presented isolated and sometimes unconnected situations. It was called *stationendrama*, and it consisted of a juxtaposition of powerful images.

The sets built on stage weren't a simulation of reality. They were abstract compositions, and the final sense was ultimately given by the audience and the ideas that resonated within them after the play. The same overlapping of scenes that structured the play was reproduced in the scenography. The sets presented a series of images placed at irregular angles. The walls that were recreated on stage seemed to crash on the actors. The set wasn't where the action happened, but it was a dramatic force (Izenour, n.d.).

The role and features of actors were also altered due to the influence of expressionism. In the late years of the 19th century and the early 20th century, the image of the director arose and replaced the actor-manager role. After this, the composition of the play was the result of the director's vision. The director assembled all the elements encompassed in the performance.

One of those directors was Edward Gordon Craig, who claimed that actors couldn't help ruining the fantasy created on stage. Unlike realism and naturalism, actors weren't asked to reproduce reality but to persuade the spectators that everything performed on stage was an illusion (Lewis, n.d.d). As a stage designer, Craig liked to use light to create suggestive environments to help create such effects.

Craig worked with and was inspired by the German expressionist Wagner. He is credited with being the father of theater lighting. Craig's first play was *Dido and Aeneas*, performed at the Purcell Operatic Society in 1900. He rejected using rows of lights, instead adding structures that would change the projection of the light behind the proscenium. This allowed the director to create innumerable perspectives.

Chapter 7
The Golden Age of Musicals

As explained in previous chapters, music was a common element in theater. First, through the music hall presentations and the operas, especially during the time of the Licensing Act, and second, as a resource to create special effects. In the 20th century, a new fusion between music and theatrical performance originated a distinctive theatrical genre: musicals.

Musical use elements of the opera, ballet, vaudeville, and burlesque genres. Its origins can be traced back to antiquity, though the first musical in history was *The Black Crook*, which opened on Broadway, New York, in 1866. In Great Britain, musicals were mainly shaped by the works of Gilbert and Sullivan.

In the 19th century, there was a mutual influence between the theatrical movement that concentrated on Broadway in the United States and London's West End. Many plays that premiered in the West End were later taken to Broadway or vice versa. Nonetheless, theatrical activity declined in the first half of the 20th century. The two world wars and the complex scenario of the interwar period discouraged investors, and the fall in the working-class income cut down the attendance rates. In addition, the appearance and evolution of the film industry created a new competitor to theatrical companies.

The similarities to modern Broadway musicals can be found in the 1920s and 1930s musical comedies, where lyrics and music were composed for the plays. *Show Boat* by Kern and Hammerstein was the first play to blend music as a plot component. Music was completely integrated in 1943 with the presentation of *Oklahoma!*

At the beginning of the 1940s, theater entered the Golden Age. It opened with the premiere of what is considered the first modern musical: *Oklahoma!* The musical premiered in 1943, produced by Rodgers and Hammerstein, and reached a fantastic record of 2,212 performances. The show set the new basis for musicals and continues to have a long influence on both sides of the Atlantic.

Oklahoma! was a play with musical pieces, but unlike the preceding plays with music, the lyrics of the songs were used as additional dialogue. So, the songs contributed to telling the story. The dancing wasn't an accessory; Instead, the moves were used as dramatic instruments. The ballet or group of dancers accompanying the main characters represented the unspoken thoughts or emotions that completed the essence of the picture.

This musical was exported from Broadway to the London West End in 1947. It premiered at the Royal Theater on Drury Lane on April 30th. It was welcomed by theater-goers and critics and completed the unprecedented record of 1,543 performances. It was the first of many musicals that traveled west to east during the post-war years.

The Rise of Musical Theater in the Early 20th Century

Musicals were first developed in the American theater district of Broadway. Theater in America started developing in the 17th century but was banned by the conservative morality of U.S. society. Theatrical activity eventually developed in the 19th century, but, at first, companies came from Europe, mainly Great Britain, to present their productions. Actors and playwrights went from the old continent, searching for new opportunities. In the early decades of the 20th century, that flow changed direction.

There was a Golden Age between the outbreak of World War II and the 1970s. During that period, over 100 plays were taken from Broadway to the West End in London (Hathaway, 2013). The first musical performed in the West End was called *Wild Rose*, though its Broadway original version was called *Sally*. *Wild Rose* premiered in 1942, and it was the beginning of musical success in the West End, similar to the phenomenon happening on Broadway.

Musical plays, revues, and musical comedies in London in the 1920s and 1930s met great success compared to their compatriots in other important European capitals. One of the reasons is related to the history of theater in London. Moreover, London was always a cosmopolitan city that embraced modernity, new inventions, and the commercialization of fashion and cultural products before the other big continental cities. It was the perfect atmosphere for an innovative and fresh theater genre.

Isaac Q. Miller

Iconic Musical Productions and Their Legacies

The first memorable musical play in London—before the appearance of modern musicals in 1943—was *The Arcadians*. Ambient and Thompson wrote it, Wimperis wrote the lyrics, and Monckton and Talbot composed the music. It premiered in 1909 at the Shaftesbury Theater. It performed in the West End for three years and was presented on 809 occasions. It was also taken to Broadway in 1910 with a new American cast (Platt & Becker, 2013).

Other iconic comedies and vaudeville plays of the first decades of the 20th century were *Quality Street*, *The Catch of the Season*, *The Girl in the Train*, and *The Cherry Girl*. All of them were presented in London's West End between 1901 and 1911. The main themes revolved around simple romantic stories of ordinary characters, mainly belonging to the working class.

Chapter 8
Theater and the World Wars

Contrary to what might be thought at first, theaters and the entertainment business didn't halt due to the war. In fact, they became essential in Great Britain. Theater played a series of roles during the wars, most notably to keep up the morale of the population at home and the soldiers on the front. It was used to promote patriotic feelings and provide a light distraction to citizens. The revenues were used to fund the war expenses.

World War II started for Great Britain on September 3rd, 1939. That night, war was declared on Germany. The following day, Prime Minister Chamberlain announced the closure of theaters, but it only lasted a few months. It was the worst conflict the country had been involved in, and still, theaters remained open. The play *Sunny River* was performed 86 times in 1943 at Piccadilly Theater in London. That is a clear example of what going to the theater meant for Londoners, even in war.

Isaac Q. Miller

The Impact of the World Wars on Theater Production

The situation of Great Britain was different in both world wars. World War II had deeper and longer-lasting effects since the conflict persisted for more time than World War I. Nonetheless, some main traits were similar regarding the reaction of theater people—those involved in the industry and theatergoers—and theater's role during the war.

Before the outbreak of the war, the London theater district was the pinnacle of theater in Europe. Companies and actors from all over the world came to the West End to perform, and there was an intense and rich cultural exchange that contributed to the modernization of the plays. By the beginning of the 20th century, Broadway in New York became the epicenter of theater for many, but London's West End still was the real capital of the world since it was the greatest pole of attraction for performers and playwrights (Eustace & Parke, n.d.).

When Great Britain entered World War I on August 4th, all that momentum stopped. At first, the government reduced the presence of people in the streets and public spaces, fearing potential attacks. Nonetheless, soon, regular activity returned, and theaters and all the other entertainment activities were allowed.

The scenario was different during World War II. While the reaction of the government and people was similar to the previous conflict at first, on September 7th, the Blitz began. It was a sustained air attack over London that lasted 57 consecutive nights. Over 40,000 civilians died, and the bombs destroyed houses and buildings in the center of cities. The West End was one of the most affected areas. The Queens Theater and the Piccadilly Theater were turned into ruins, and other theaters suffered significant damage. Even so, many theaters remained open (Britannica The Wars deeply impacted theater activity, but it didn't stop shows. In hindsight, war-theater has been criticized for the quality of the productions and the lascivious and vulgar content taken on stage. These opinions contrast the productions during the war with the high works of the Edwardian' golden age.' None of the critics can be separated from the complex context where it developed. Despite the adversities, the industry managed to survive. It was a prolific period, and, most importantly, the theater played a series of critical roles within a society hit by the horrors of war.

Theatrical productions during the World Wars encompassed musicals, traditional plays, revues, concerts, and music hall shows. Professional actors and actresses shared the stage with amateurs. Managers were more concerned about keeping the business alive and giving it continuity than keeping up with artistic trends. In addition to this, everybody committed to doing their share to help in the cause of the nation.

During the war, theater companies faced an extensive list of challenges. First, theaters had to close the days that followed the declaration of war. It coincided with the theatrical season on both occasions, so companies had already arranged their shows. Most of them couldn't even premier or had to close after a few presentations. About a month after the declaration of war, theaters reopened. However, attendance at the shows was limited by the limited availability of public transport. The state had put the railways at the service of the army's needs. In addition, even after people overcame the fear of being attacked, the average income was barely enough to survive.

On the other hand, many members of the companies'

crews were enlisted to join the army. At first, there was no compulsory conscription, but about 800 men involved in theatrical activities (performers, playwrights, designers, musicians, and more) volunteered to go to the battlefront (Eustace & Parke, n.d.). Companies proceeded the best they could by replacing their cast with new people.

During certain periods of the war, like October 1914 during World War I, the government passed the decision to darken the city during the night as a preventive measure in case of air bombarding. This didn't discourage theater people. Although evening activities decreased, they experimented with matinees earlier in the afternoons.

British people's spirit was strong, and they soon became accustomed to the new living conditions, and theater continued. In December 1914, the first Christmas under a World War, 26 theaters were open at the West End, only three less than the previous season (Eustace & Parke, n.d.).

Even though people preserved their enthusiasm for theater, the economic conditions of the war forced most of the population to reduce their expenditures, especially on those items that weren't necessary. The managers searched for a way to lower the prices for people from all social segments. To achieve that, they were forced to reduce the costs, which soon reflected in actors' and stagehands' salaries. People's income was barely above subsistence levels. Hence, managers and theater employees had to call for help from the Actors Benevolent Fund and the Actors Emergency War Fund.

Theater companies had very little support from the government. While they were allowed to open, there was no economic relief. On the contrary, theaters had to pay higher and more taxes during both wars. Most theater managers kept their business at a loss. Then, why did they do it?

During the war, every citizen wanted to do their part to support those fighting on the front. Theater managers, performers, and all the other employees knew that theater had a vital role.

The plays presented on stage represented life on the battlefield and told the stories of brave soldiers. It not only burst national pride but also encouraged civilians to volunteer, cooperate, and support the government. Theater performances were also a means to promote recruitment and raise funds for hospitals and the army.

The theater was also one of the leading resources to keep up the troops' morale and the population. Theater was a way to escape from the terrible reality. Such was the importance of theater as a way to keep the audience amused and calm while the world was on fire, and the censorship office of Lord Chamberlain loosened some of the restrictions.

Along with all the economic challenges faced by theater managers, they had to struggle with censorship. During the wars, the Lord Chamberlain's office eventually allowed managers to present plays with sexual references or other taboo topics. Nonetheless, censorship was still strong in political affairs.

Theatrical performances were also taken to the front lines. It was a remedy for boredom and a way to soften fear and long for home. Back in the country, the theater was also an entertainment resource for all those involved in the war industry and confined to the recruitment centers.

Last but not least, the theater was also the space to funnel social discontent for being at war, the harsh conditions, and all social inequalities that existed before the war but had only deepened through the conflict. Some plays that had been banned in the past for the moral inaccuracy of their content were now allowed. For instance, Oscar Wilde's *Salome*, with an exotic and sensual performance by Noel Pemberton, *Billing MP*, and Henrik Ibsen's *Ghosts*, which had been rejected by the critics when the independent theater company performed it, now all found a spot on stage (Maunder et al., 2015). People were excited to attend the "for adults only" plays, and the censorship office chose to look the other way. They had other urgent issues to attend to.

The Influence of War on Theatrical Themes and Aesthetics

The war-time theater was poorly valued in the following years. George Bernard Shaw said plays written and adapted during those years were silly entertainment. Stories lacked content, and the plots depicted smiling and vulnerable soldiers. In sum, they only provided the idea of being happy just because fire had ceased (Maunder et al., 2015).

While the number of plays and performances during the years of war was high, there were indeed several changes in the aesthetics of the performances and the sets. There was a halt in the evolutionary line that the British theater had followed. The predominant trends led by realism and naturalism at the beginning of the 20th century were paused, and they wouldn't return until the end of WWII, where, even still, they had changed forever. The theater reflected society and reacted to the changes and new demands.

The changes in the aesthetics and the narrative styles resulted from many factors. One of them was the decrease of the budget to put a play on stage. There was less money to invest in scenography, lighting, and costumes. Another problem was that many professional actors had to leave their jobs at the theater to join the army. Therefore, many amateur performers reached the major stages of the West End, and their performances weren't always as superb as those of the distinguished stars of the previous period. Anyway, people weren't searching for excellence or realism. They just wanted to have some fun and forget there was a violent war beyond the theater doors.

The themes covered by the plays were slightly different from the Victorian melodrama. Most stories were about fleeting and common issues, often in scenarios associated with the war. Some of the most famous plays were *The Man Who Stayed at Home, The Merry Wives of Windsor, Seven Days Leave, The Scarlet Pimpernel,* and *The Female Hun* (Maunder et al., 2015). Even though these plays treated real-life affairs, the aesthetics were far different from the realism and naturalism of the pre-war time.

Musical plays and revues were the most popular. Some of the most remarkable and long-running musicals were *Chu Chin Chow*, with 2,238 performances, and *The Maid of the Mountains*, with 1,352 performances. The most popular revues were *Shell Out* and *The Big Boys Are Here*, with over 300 performances each, and *Zig Zag*, with almost 650 performances (Maunder et al., 2015).

It is interesting to notice that not all the pre-war theater disappeared in these years. For instance, the professional actors of the Edwardian period, John Leslie Isaacson and J.G. Pockets, continued to perform. Instead of the major stages, they organized amateur presentations at a hospital in Glasgow. George Bernard Shaw, a harsh critic of the war-period theater, contributed several scripts: *O'Flaherty, Augustus Does His Bit,* and *Heartbreak House.* The great actor Laurence Olivier had his first success in the West End in the inter-war period in the play *Private Lives* by Noël Coward. Other significant actors debuted in this context: John Gielgud, Vivien Leigh, and Alec Guinness, to name a few. The theater also became a place of opportunities, especially for women who entered the business and managed their own companies.

Despite the ups and downs, the time between World Wars (1914-1945) was fertile and enabled new aesthetics and narratives to flourish and thrive in the post-war period. Theater during those convulsive years is now considered a bridge between the past before the horror and the future that started when it was all over. It reflects a moment in history that hurts to remember. The most significant aspect to point out is the versatility, sense of duty, and commitment of all those who were involved in one way or another with the business.

Chapter 9

Modern West End

The world after WWII had little in common with the one before 1914. Somehow, it was a new beginning for humankind. It was also the rebirth of everything, including theater. Some of the elements of theater previous to the outbreak of war were reintegrated, and some were reshaped to meet the expectations of new audiences, all while reflecting their current reality. The desires had changed. The way to look at reality and into the future was different. Theater and arts, in general, searched for the best way to mirror that on stage.

After World War II, the world had to be rebuilt in every possible sense. The aftermath of the conflict was an unprecedented number of casualties, uncountable economic losses, and extreme levels of destruction in the cities. Even though the damages in Great Britain were far less than in the rest of Europe, London wasn't an exception to this critical scenario. A fifth part of the theaters in the West End were utterly destroyed or seriously damaged. The budgets to mount a show had increased, and the government had implemented a new tax on entertainment events.

It was a difficult time to run a business in the entertainment industry. As it had happened in the 17th century, a group of theater managers had a monopoly in the West End once more. They preferred secure blockbusters, plays that would be sure successes. Therefore, most plays were thrillers, light comedies, and musicals imported from Broadway.

In these conditions, the theater had to deal with the challenges of rebuilding the whole infrastructure and finding a new place in society. By the 1940s and 1950s, other mass communication media had spread. The entertainment business was then swamped with productions from more developed and refined movie, radio, and television industries. The theater had to find something unique to offer an audience that had many alternatives.

The Rise of Experimental and Avant Garde Theater

The years post-war formed a favorable scenario to experiment with new aesthetics and genres. In theater, new movements gained the center of the scene. One of those movements was the experimental theater, also known as avant-garde. The avant-garde was a way to shake the archaic structures of the status quo and resist traditional theater. The keys were innovation and experimentation. The only rule was that there were no rules.

In general terms, the avant-garde dates from the 19th century, when the term was first used. It referred to the potential of theater and arts to spread new ideas and social change. In the Western theater, the representatives of realism and naturalism were considered part of this movement. The works of Ibsen and Chekhov can be regarded as the avant-garde of the 19th century.

In the 20th century, experimental theater—the avant-garde—mainly used the contributions of Bertolt Brecht. The playwright believed it wasn't enough to recreate reality on stage. He considered that the artist could never ultimately persuade the audience of the illusion of theater. He wanted to go further and engage the spectators in a transforming experience. It was the audience's job to discover the meaning of what was said on stage. It was a sort of surrealist theater where the performers suggested a scene and provided the elements, but it was the viewers who put the pieces together and created the story.

In the West End, Bretch's works influenced renowned playwrights such as Edward Bond, Caryl Churchill, and John Arden. The Royal Shakespeare Company also followed Bretch's concepts in some of their plays. In the 1950s, experimental theater continued to develop. Joan Littlewood, a theater manager, was particularly interested in this new writing style. She owned the Theatre Workshop, which targeted a working-class audience, and later moved to the Theatre Roya. She presented plays that included several fragments left for improvisation by the performers. The play *Oh, What a Lovely War!* performed in 1963 is an example.

The changes in the performance demanded actors and actresses with a background and skills to embody the new type of characters. The traditional, sophisticated actors with polished lines performed for an upper-class audience were replaced with actors and actresses who spoke to an audience expected to continue internally the dialogues and the reasonings presented on stage. The play was just a catalyst for people's emotions and thoughts about the issues covered.

The theater of the absurd emerged within the avant-garde movement of the post-war period. Expressionism had attempted to avoid reality, cut the strings with objective things, and dive into human beings' minds and souls. The theater of the absurd was also a challenge to realism and naturalism since it rejected the purpose of depicting reality to unravel it.

The theater of the absurd is based on the idea that existence and the human condition don't have a special meaning. The concept of absurdity was taken from the existentialist philosopher Albert Camus. It isn't hard to understand the relationship between the feeling of living absurd lives after the horrors of the war.

During the 1960s, theater recovered its role of embodying social protest. A wave of political unrest and social mobilization burst worldwide, including in Europe. The avant-garde emerged as an alternative culture. In Great Britain, it eventually led to the abolition of the Lord Chamberlain's office and the end of censorship.

The Evolution of Theater in the Post-War Period

Theater after the end of WWII had enough room for all artistic movements. While the avant-garde continued to evolve, other more traditional plays returned to the West End stages. During the decades that followed the war, theaters were rebuilt and restored, and plays and musicals were produced in theater clubs. It was also a way to evade censorship, at least until 1968, when censorship was finally abolished.

Many theatergoers were eager to discover new storytelling techniques and experience theater in a more active way. Many others simply searched for high-quality entertainment. In the 1940s and 1950s, musicals from Broadway like *Oklahoma!* and *Bless the Bride* were welcomed by an audience with some knowledge about theatrical shows and a desire for quality plays.

Meanwhile, other industries in the entertainment business continued to develop and improve. Because of the evolution of movies, radio, and television, theater managers wanted to explore different ways to compete and cooperate with the new media.

During the 1950s and 1960s, many West End performers and playwrights initiated their careers in drama plays adapted for the radio or BBC productions. Caryl Churchill started with radio drama, presenting the play *The Ants* in 1962. In 1973, her job was recognized by the Royal Court Theater. Joe Orton, John Mortimer, and Tom Stoppard also had their debuts on the radio. Other plays were adapted for television. *The Dock Brief* and *What Shall We Tell Caroline?* were broadcast by the BBC before being taken to the theater.

The post-war period also witnessed the emergence of national theater companies such as The National Theater Company. It was formed by the direction of Laurence Olivier in 1963.

In addition to the new traditions on stage, alternative theaters emerged. The Red Ladder and the Women's Theater Group were the two feminist companies in London's West End. In a context where political content was depicted on stages again, they questioned the predominant male presence in director and playwright roles.

One of the many innovations in British theater was the "kitchen sink realism" developed in the 1950s and 1960s. This artistic movement emerged from the work of John

Bratby, an expressionist painter. The movement didn't only reach theater but also movies, literature, and television. They attempted to represent people disillusioned with modern society who were called "angry young men." It was a metaphor for what they symbolized: anger for anything society promised and didn't give. It was also the name the members of the movement used to introduce themselves.

The kitchen sink realism movement retrieved many elements of 19th-century realism and depicted scenes from daily life, mainly of working-class people. They were concerned about the social and political conflicts of the time. Terence Rattigan, Noël Coward. John Osborne, Arnold Wesker, and Nell Dunn are some names of the kitchen sink realism movement.

The group of Angry Men and another alternative movement called "in yer face theater" in the same trend continued to develop in the following decades. Their confrontational style provoked the audience by appealing to their sensibility. It was a deep exploration of the human condition and a harsh criticism of contemporary society (V&A, n.d.).

The Integration of Multimedia Elements in Theatrical Productions

Since the appearance and increasing success of movies, theater managers had no choice but to learn from them about what the audiences wanted to see. The parallel between London's West End and America's Broadway saw how Hollywood developed into its main competitor and searched for a way to make it its best ally. The outcome was several intense collaborations between theater playwrights, composers, directors, and theater managers. The total

How the West End Became the West End

outcome was a win-win relationship. The blockbuster musicals were the long-term result of that collaboration to find a new product and a new genre to captivate the audience.

Things worked similarly in the West End. After the difficult times of the war, the theater needed to be reinvigorated and rebuilt. During the war, managers sustained the activities just for a sense of duty, without getting enough revenue to cover the costs. With the war over, they needed to focus again on making the theater a profitable business.

In the post-war period, commercial theater gained center stage because productions were costly, and the companies didn't have a loose budget. They had to make shows that would sell to survive.

Theatrical performers pursued higher incomes, so they moved to places with better salaries and bigger possibilities. Many of them became TV stars. The West End productions had a low moment in the 1950s.

During the last years of the 1960s and the 1970s, theater went through a period of decline. The entertainment industry had turned to television and filmmaking. Social discontent and revolutionary impulses were funneled through music, especially with the emergence of rock' n' roll.

In the 1980s, theater managers started introducing more visual effects to capture the audience's attention. Presenting high-quality literary pieces or deep treaties on meaningful issues wasn't enough anymore. The audience wanted to be dazzled. Almost a century before, special effects were used to reproduce reality as faithfully as possible. Now, visual effects are used to make the audience live an experience beyond the limits of reality.

The new sets and plays introduced combined music, movement, and speech in a completely innovative way.

There was a greater interest in creating striking scenographies and adding energetic choreographies to the plays. Many old plays were revived with versions that added a series of visual elements, much to the delight of viewers.

The theater companies developed presentations that blurred the boundaries between the audience and the stage. Once, the arch at the front of the stage had divided the two realms to build the idea of fantasy. Now, that division was eliminated to give the audience a more immersive experience.

The Globalization of West End Theater

The evolution of theater in the West End during the last decades of the 20th century was greatly influenced by its interaction with other cultures. This was a result of the intense globalization process that deepened after the end of WWII and accelerated in the 1980s and 1990s.

The use of innovative visual effects was inspired by Japanese theater and the Theater du Soleil, directed by Adrienne Mnouchkine in Paris. Many contributions came to Great Britain from its colonies, and the cultural exchange intensified during and after the decolonization process. Chinese and Japanese theater have influenced British managers and playwrights since the early decades of the 20th century. As globalization shortened the distances, that process could only become more significant.

New technology allowed the creators to know the trends in other places and what people enjoyed at the theater. The advanced means of transportation allowed people to take stuff and machinery abroad at cheaper prices and in less time. It also allowed the companies' crews to take international tours. If once there was a one-way path for plays, particularly musicals, from Broadway to the West End, those paths multiplied and became multidirectional thanks to globalization.

The last phenomenon enabled by globalization is called McTheater. In simple terms, it implies that theater plays have become a commodity that can be exported and imported regarding economic interests. There is a long list of plays that encompass *Cats*, which premiered at New London Theater in 1981; *Starlight Express*, which premiered at Apollo Victoria Theater in 198; and *The Phantom of the Opera*, which premiered at Her Majesty's Theater in 1986, just to name a few. All of them are initially from the West End, but the list is enlarged with other Broadway blockbusters.

The concept of McTheater means these theater productions are a commercial franchise. The critics point out that it goes against the fundamental purposes of theater and reduces art to a commercial good. The term McTheater has a pejorative connotation, a way to point out that type of play as lower quality, only motivated by financial interests. This judgmental perspective ignores that "McTheater" enabled theater to be a highly profitable business and would encourage more and better productions. Therefore, more plays could be taken abroad, and more people worldwide could attend and enjoy them. It is simply another way to make the entertainment business grow.

Chapter 10
West End Icons And Legends

The history of the London West End was written by the talent and efforts of many people who dedicated their lives to theater—actors who weren't just in charge of bringing to life fictional characters. For centuries, actors were also the managers of the companies who had to make decisions, own the theaters, and run a business. Their role was key to the development of the entertainment industry.

It is impossible to summarize in a chapter or even in one book all the outstanding names that helped build the West End and make it the world capital of theater. Nonetheless, we will attempt to honor some of the most remarkable names. Those icons whose performances created a new style, gave performing arts new concepts, and left enduring legacies.

In the 20th century, directors gained importance with the unparalleled mission of assembling all the elements of a show under a unique vision. Music, acting, lights, scenography, and choreographies contributed to telling the story and leading the audience to an unforgettable experience. These individuals have also steered the course in the West End and performing arts in the world.

Celebrating Iconic Performers of the West End

Ellen Terry

She was born to a family of actors on February 27, 1847. Her career developed during the Victorian era, and her name is associated with the great names of the time. She debuted with Charles Kean at the Princess's Theatre when she was only nine years old. Later, actor Henry Irving, manager of the Lyceum Theater, made her the leading star of the company. Her most memorable performances were embodying Shakespearean characters, but she is also remembered as a comedian actress. She performed in *The Merchant of Venice* and was Ophelia in *Othello*.

Ellen evolved from the theater and left melodramas to join the social realism stream. She left Irving's company and started working with George Bernard Shaw. Ellen became a manager herself. She directed the Imperial Theater in the early 20th century and produced Ibsen's *The Vikings* and Shakespeare's *Much Ado About Nothing*. The scenography was created by her son, George Craig, the leader in the innovation of set design.

Mrs. Patrick Campbell

Her real name was Beatrice Rose Stella Tanner, but everybody knew her by her stage name, Mrs. Patrick Campbell, or simply Mrs. Pat. Her first appearance in the London

West End was at the Adelphi Theater in 1890. Soon, she performed at the most famous theaters in the district.

Her career took off when the director George Bernard Shaw became interested in her. In 1897, he tried to include her as the star in *The Devil's Disciple*, but Mrs. Pat didn't accept the part. Many years later, Mrs. Patrick Campbell finally decided to work with Shaw. She was the leading actress in the famous play *Pygmalion*. That role launched her as a national star. Mrs. Pat and Shaw had a mutual fascination and an intense romantic relationship.

Her acting style was shaped by her charming looks and expressive voice. She is remembered for daring to play controversial and unconventional roles. She performed Mrs. Tanqueray and Mrs. Ebbsmith, two characters that questioned the place of women in society and the conventions about marriage.

Mrs. Pat was one of the West End actresses who continued to the big screen. She worked in several movies, such as *Crime and Punishment* and *Mooney Moon*.

Dame Judi Dench

Her name is associated with the greatest plays written by Shakespeare. Judi Dench played Ophelia in *Othello*, Juliet in *Romeo and Juliet*, and Lady Macbeth in *Macbeth*. Her career started in 1957 at the Old Vic Company.

In the 1960s, she became a movie star but never walked away from the theater. She had a prolific career in the movie industry and is widely known for her role as M in *James Bond* and the leading role as Queen Victoria in *Mrs. Brown*.

In 2006, she joined the Royal Shakespeare Company to play a role in *The Merry Wives of Windsor*. Later, she also starred in *A Midsummer Night's Dream* at the Rose Theater and *Madame de Sade* at the Wyndham's Theater.

Her name stands out for her long-lasting career of over 60 years. Judi Dench is an accomplished actress on the West End and Broadway, and she has proved her versatility by performing roles in tragedies and musicals.

Laurence Olivier

He is considered the best actor of his generation. He performed the most famous roles in the history of theater and memorable novel characters on stage and for movies and television. He was Hamlet, Henry V, Richard III, King Lear, and Heathcliff in the epic *Wuthering Heights*.

Sir Laurence Olivier had his early debut at the age of nine at a school play. He was Brutus in Shakespeare's *Julius Caesar*. It was the first of the many plays written by Shakespeare that he would star in. His first appearance in the West End was with the play *Beau Geste*.

Even though his name is closely associated with the British stages and the London West End, Olivier also had a brilliant career in Broadway and Hollywood.

His career wasn't limited to being a multi-awarded actor. He was also a celebrated director. He directed the movie *The Prince and the Showgirl* (1957) with Marilyn Monroe and adapted the film *Uncle Vanya* and *Three Sisters* for television. He proves the common interchange between the different industries within the entertainment business and how the talent of actors and directors helped the industry's development.

The Influence of Notable Directors on the West End Stage

Edward Gordon Craig

His name has been mentioned several times in the chapters when speaking about the evolution of theater in the 20th century. Edward Gordon Craig was a pioneer of his time, and his work was a milestone in theater.

He started his career as an actor but succeeded as a playwright, producer, and director. At the beginning of the 20th century, he started implementing his approach to create the set for realism. He had revolutionary ideas about theatrical design. Craig chose simple scenographies, and the effects were mainly achieved through the use of lights that followed the actors on stage to mark the moments of the story.

In 1907, he worked with Konstantin Stanislavsky, the creator of a new acting technique that would also revolutionize theater. Stanislavsky's method consisted of special training of actors to dominate their bodies and understand the deep motivations of the characters to better reflect their emotions when performing on stage. Craig and Stanislavsky together created a whole new concept within performing arts. Reality wasn't depicted as it is but as a symbolic recreation.

Joan Littlewood

Littlewood left a significant footprint in the London West End. Although many of her works were first presented outside the West End, she eventually directed plays at the most important stages of the theatrical district. Her most famous work is the 1963 play *Oh, What a Lovely War!*.

She pioneered new ways of management, earning her the title "the mother of modern theater." The Theater Workshop, founded by Littlewood, was run with egalitarian foundations, and the productions were created in collaboration with the members of the company. It started outside London in 1953 when the company started working at the East End theaters. Some years later, Littlewood and her company reached the West End.

Binkie Beaumont and H.M. Tennent

Together, Binkie Beaumont and H.M. Tennent are clear examples of the situation of the theater during wartime and the years that followed. They were men of business, and their main concern was to make theater a growing and profitable business. Some people criticized them for that, but they were vital to keeping the industry alive because they were able to understand the circumstances and adapt to them. In 1939, after World War II broke out and the Lord Chamberlain's office ordered the theaters to shut down, Beaumont used his influence to allow them to open again.

In a context when social realism and the new trends flooded the market, Beaumont and Tennet offered a more traditional version of theater, presenting classic plays such as *The Importance of Being Earnest* and *Hamlet*. They claimed these plays had an educational purpose and obtained a government subsidiary to help support the company. This gave them a commercial advantage over the competition.

As West End producers, they worked with recognized playwrights of the time: Vivien Leigh, Victor Spinetti, Nöel

Coward, Richard Burton, Ivor Novello, and Ingrid Bergman. *West Side Story* and *My Fair Lady* are some of their most remembered productions.

Sir Peter Hall

Peter Hall is considered one of the most influential people in British theater. Among his many contributions, we must name founding the Royal Shakespeare Company and transforming the National Theater into a competitive and prestigious institution.

Sir Peter Hall was a celebrated theater director, but he also had a career in the movie industry and directed pieces for television. He has an extensive list of successful plays in the West End and outside, including plays starring outstanding names such as Laurence Olivier.

He is better remembered for the creation of the Shakespeare Company in the city where the playwright was born, Stratford-upon-Avon, in 1961. He brought the epic classical plays back to the stage with a modern and innovative stage design and added all the new acting techniques. He was a master of assembling old texts with contemporary designs to create a fresh technique style.

The London West End's Longest-Run Plays in the 20th Century

The Mousetrap

This is the longest-running play of the West End and in the world. It has been performed nearly 29,000 times and counting (Statista, 2023).

It is based on the thriller novel written by Agatha Christie. It was first written to be performed as a radio drama play requested by the BBC and originally was called *Three Blind Mice.*

It premiered at the Theatre Royal, Nottingham, on October 6, 1952. It was presented in many theaters in Great Britain until it reached London in November of that year. The play was performed at the Ambassadors Theater. Through over 70 years of history, The Mousetrap has been presented in other theaters and toured in countries all over the world, including Australia, China, and Singapore.

Les Misérables

This is the second longest-running play of the West End. An original story written by Victor Hugo in the 19th century, it has been taken to the stage and the big screen with several versions. More than 130 million people have seen the West End production; it was presented in 53 countries and translated into 22 languages (Les Misérables London-Official Web Site, 2023).

It is a musical written by Schönberg and Boublil. The music was composed by Claude-Michel Schönberg, and the lyrics belong to Alain Boublil and Jean-Marc Nate. The original play premiered in Paris in 1980 and was presented in London in October 1985 under the direction of Cameron Mackintosh. Herbert Kretzmer made the English version of the lyrics.

It is the longest-running musical of the West End and the second longest in the world, only preceded by the off-Broadway show *The Fantasticks.*

The Phantom of the Opera

This musical is based on the homonymous novel written in 1910 by Gaston Leroux. The script was written by Andrew Lloyd Webber and Stilgoe, the music was by Webber, and the lyrics were by Charles Hart. It tells the story of an opera singer who falls in love with a mysterious musical talent who lives beneath the Paris Opera House and wears a mask.

The play premiered at Her Majesty's Theater in the West End in 1986, and in 1988, it was also taken to Broadway. It is one of the most successful plays of all time, with over six billion dollars in revenues. The show closed in the West End due to the COVID-19 pandemic in 2020. It reopened in 2021 but eventually presented the last show on April 16, 2023.

Cats

The musical *Cats* is based on poems by T.S. Eliot, which were written in the 1930s. It tells the story of felines called Jellicle Cats. It opened in the New London Theater in the West End in 1981. It also opened at the Winter Garden Theater on Broadway the following year. The play has popular songs like "Macavity: The Mystery Cat," "Jellicle Song for Jellicle Cats," and "Memory."

The original West End play performed for 21 years and over 8,000 presentations. On Broadway, it remained on stage for 18 years. It stopped in 2002 and was revived twice in London West End. In 2023, it came on stage again at the London Palladium for limited presentations.

Chapter 11

Contemporary Trends and Innovations

During the last decades, there have been a lot of changes in the world that have directly impacted the performing arts. Once, technological progress was used to create more realistic designs. The broadening of the audience from all different social sectors encouraged managers and playwrights to explore new ways to tell stories. The appearance of mass media communication presented a challenge to theater companies. Eventually, it led to collaboration between the different realms and the evolution of the entertainment industry.

Nonetheless, the evolution of technology, digital applications, and artificial intelligence introduces an entirely different problem compared to the past. The audience can access a wide and varied offering of shows, and it is even harder to impress them. It puts new challenges in front of producers from all around the world but also a wide range of possibilities. How will theater at the London West End find the quintessence that makes their content unique and irreplaceable for people? What are the resources to make theater the best to watch among the many other options?

The Diversification of Theater Genres and Styles

Many things have changed since the emergence of expressionism and experimental theater. In the second half of the 20th century, the line between fiction and reality was already blurred. The distance between the theatergoers and what happened on stage had been reshaped. Those who used only to be audience members assumed a more active role. They engaged in building the final meaning of what was being performed. In the 21st century, the audiences go further.

The new trends had to turn everything that was known around. The buildings where the theater was presented were always paramount. It is much more than the auditorium with seats and a stage. It creates the environment for magic—or reality—to take place. Therefore, contemporary theaters are being rebuilt and reshaped under the new concepts of design, which are extensions of current trends and styles.

Some time ago, the idea of theaters was the black box: an environment of pure neutrality. Directors wanted to present their productions in sterilized spaces where the performers built all the form and substance—the meaning. The new theaters follow new maximalist aesthetics that might be the outcome of original combinations of different styles. Eclecticism is the rule.

The new trends demand a theater that is in a direct, constant relationship with what happens around it. These recent trends impact stories and characters and also the building designs. People want to go to a theater where they feel comfortable—a place they find familiar.

The changes in the concept of what theater is have taken the performing arts even outside the theaters. Companies or simple groups of actors can mount a show anywhere, and it is still cherished as theater. The space is no longer limited to the structures of the buildings. The theatrical district is following the pace of this new trend, creating open-air spaces for performances, sometimes as a continuation of the inner stage.

The Impact of Site-Specific and Immersive Experiences

A new type of theater has emerged in the last couple of decades. It is called site-specific theater. It proposes more immersive productions that allow the audiences to have hands-on shows, enjoying and giving sense to what is presented on stage and performing more concrete actions. The imaginary fourth wall between the audience and the actors no longer exists.

Many features that can be added to the shows are only possible because of digital development. New technologies such as VR (virtual reality), AR (augmented reality), and MR (mixed reality) have ended the three-dimensional reality we were used to. It is becoming more common in our daily lives, and its presence is gaining importance in every realm. The theater isn't an exception.

These new technologies bring unlimited possibilities for storytelling to the theater but put new challenges on playwrights who need to integrate those resources into their stories. Even though the rules for using them are currently being written, it is fair to expect that every new element will join the others to create a unit: the play. It is also a challenge for directors and producers who must assemble more elements and, of course, for actors.

Special effects have been used in theater for ages, as explained before. Nonetheless, this is the first time in history when technological devices can literally create reality or alter it instead of just making an illusion. Producers and designers are experimenting with automated speech recognition to translate what is said on stage in real-time. This would involve the audience's smartphones (Brook, 2016).

Other innovative ways exist to introduce new technologies and make the plays more interactive. For instance, people in the audience can use their smartphones to change the end of the story.

The emergence of more simultaneous platforms to display the shows is another innovation. The use of multiple platforms spread during the COVID-19 pandemic when theaters had to close, but companies needed to make money. Then, plays were taken from stages to on-demand platforms. At present, a multiplatform system is attractive but still not cost-efficient. The producers and managers know the benefits of reaching a broader audience. However, the implementation details are still under development (Brook, 2016).

The Ethical Considerations of Technology in Theater

Besides the economic odds of developing and introducing new technologies to the productions, many ethical considerations are in the background. The use of AI and the applications of VR, AR, and MR to different aspects of our lives marches faster than our ability to process the changes these technologies encompass. Yet, the entertainment industry also faces other concerns regarding different areas.

One of the main concerns within the theatrical business is the greater impact of the activity on the environment, and sometimes, it isn't even necessary to talk about these new technologies. The facilities demanded by comfort in the contemporary era have increased environmental damage. For instance, the air-conditioning of small auditoriums has increased global warming. The improvements to project the sound inside the theaters and block the background sound from the streets also result in a high demand for resources and a high use of energy and emission of heat.

Theater people have a major concern about this issue and have committed to searching for sustainable and green designs for theaters. "Major theatres in 30 countries in Europe have committed to [sic] reduce their carbon emissions to zero by 2030 as part of a plan coordinated by the ETC" (Economist Impact, n.d., para. 9). Some measures already implemented are reducing the emission of gasses, smart use of energy, and recycling.

In recent years, more theaters have engaged in sustainable initiatives. For instance, the Arcola Theater in London set a major goal to become the first carbon-neutral theater. This goal was accomplished in 2007. It became an example of what can indeed be done. They used recycled material and installed solar panels to produce energy. They could reduce 25% of carbon emissions and replace traditional lights with LED lighting, resulting in an 89% decrease in electricity use (Economist Impact, n.d.).

The National Theater, on its end, mounted a show with 90% of the props and scenography made of recycled materials. The play was *Trouble in Mind*. The purpose isn't only to do their share in the fight to restrain climate change and global heating but also to help spread the message of social responsibility to the theatergoers. After all, every great storyteller knows the importance of 'show, don't tell'.

The Intersection of Art and Activism in Theatrical Works

The increasing concern for environmental issues isn't the only matter that involves theater with what is going on outside in the world. The theater has always been a space of intersection where society's troubles were exposed and shared. Theater has always been an essential ingredient in the process of shaping society. It has boosted changes, resisted the status quo, opened spaces for the less heard and invisible, and created opportunities for minorities.

Theater continues to be the environment where taboo and uncomfortable topics in society can be displayed. It is also a space that reveals several inequalities. It is a mirror of what happens in society. For instance, there are a low number of women in managing roles or as producers. There is also a big difference in the spaces taken by people from different economic and ethnic backgrounds. It isn't a problem reserved for theater. It is just one more space in the world where this gap exists.

Nonetheless, society isn't only discussing the inequalities within the industry and brought on stage with the plays. Blind casting is being used more and more frequently to ensure the best actors due to their talent and not just appearance. There has also been a lot more freedom for people to create the stories they want to share.

The discussion on inequalities and social responsibility is also focusing on the audience. There is an increasing concern about implementing the required amenities and accommodations to allow disabled people to enjoy a show fully. This is still a pending matter, but at least it now has a place on the agenda of changes to be made.

The West End in the 21st century – the Audience's Favorite Plays

There are 39 theaters in the West End, and deciding which shows are the best is almost impossible. The following four are a small sample of the various styles and genres that coexist in the London theater district, faithful to its great tradition.

Tina

This is a typical jukebox musical that takes the audience on an amazing trip through the life and career of one of the most beloved singers of all time, Tina Turner. The play's director is Phyllida Lloyd, the same one who brought *Mamma Mia* on stage, the bedrock of modern jukebox musicals.

The play tells the story of Tina, from her humble origins in Tennessee to her love affairs and epic comeback. Her greatest hits are, of course, included in the show. 'Proud Mary' and 'River Deep, Mountain High' aren't only hits of the '60s but of every generation of music fans.

The play premiered on April 17, 2018, at Aldwych Theatre. After two successful years, the play halted due to the lockdown during the COVID-19 pandemic. It reopened in July 2021 and became one of London's West End blockbusters.

Cabaret

One of the classics still on the West End stage, the multi-awarded *Cabaret* continues to captivate old and new generations. The story takes place at the Kit Kat Club (located in Berlin), a place where everyone can be free. However, in the outside world, fascism is rising.

The play is presented at the Playhouse Theater, located at the Convert Garden near the historic Trafalgar Square. It premiered on Broadway in 1966 and reached the West End two years later. Over the years, there have been several revivals of *Cabaret* on both sides of the Atlantic—the last revival opened in December 2021.

As theater always strives to be unique and experiment, the show doesn't start when the performers come on stage. The experience begins before. People are invited to a real night at the Kit Kat Club. Before the show, they access a club entry time with food, drinks, and a pre-show. The people who attend the play actually enter a club, with the performers acting as if they were the people from the club in real life. They believe they *are* at a club instead of being just spectators of a play.

Pygmalion

George Bernard Shaw's masterpiece continues to be a timeless success. This drama-comedy is a contemporary adaptation of the original script. It tells the story of a woman on the streets who is under the tutelage of a gentleman who will try to educate and transform her. Will he accomplish the mission?

It is performed at one of the oldest theaters in London, the Old Vic Theater. The play premiered in September

2023, although it had many revivals after its debut in Vienna in 1913 and at His Majesty's Theater in the West End in 1914.

Peter Grimes

This is an example of how all the genres have a place on West End stages. *Peter Grimes* is an English National Opera production. It is an opera of significant influence throughout the 20th century and, in the 21st century, continues to be one of the audience's preferred shows.

The play is performed at the London Coliseum, which opened in 1904. It is one of the oldest theaters in the city. It was initially a variety theater. The opera was first performed in Great Britain in 1945 at the reopening of the Sadler's Wells Theater after World War II.

Chapter 12
The Future of the West End

The last century's development taught us all to better deal with uncertainty. In the last decades, changes have accelerated, and many things seem to be happening simultaneously. Theater is the intersection where all the pieces are put together.

Nonetheless, there are still a number of odds to overcome. The key is to find the balance between recognizing the problem and taking action.

Anticipating the Challenges and Opportunities Ahead

As explained in the previous chapter, design and technological progress are revolutionizing theater. It gives the business unlimited abilities to develop and reach unimaginable levels. Nonetheless, there is a less kind side to the matter. The economic factor is widening the breach between companies with the resources to invest and innovate and those without.

The last statistics show a fall in public investment in the

private sector, to which 86% of the theater industry belongs. This has impacted the work of independent organizations. A reduced number of companies collect the highest revenues. Therefore, the wealth generated by theater continues to be concentrated on a select few.

The difference in the revenues gathered by the few major companies drastically contrasts with the modest income of the majority of minor companies: "Large organizations (51+ permanent staff) generated 78% of all Earned income, compared with 21% by medium-sized organizations (10-50 staff) and 1% by the small organizations (under 10 staff)" (Brook, 2016 p. 7).

Meanwhile, theater organizations are also innovating in the way they raise funds. Companies are implementing public funding and social investment. The government supports these initiatives with some tax relief measures and loose loans. At the same time, theaters have raised ticket prices to increase revenue—all while keeping an eye on sales that have not dropped yet.

Embracing Diversity and Inclusivity on the Stage

As exposed in the previous chapter, inclusion and diversity aren't the only matters of concern for playwrights. At present, this is an issue that goes through all aspects of the business, including the labor market associated with the theater and the audiences. According to recent reports, there are still several hot spots to work on.

The representation of people with Black, Asian, or minority ethnic (BAME) backgrounds continues to be significantly low in the audiences. This can reflect either an economic impediment to access cultural goods or a lack of interest regarding the type of content presented on stage. This particular issue demands consideration since the BAME isn't a homogeneous group, and all the particularities should be attended to (Brook, 2016).

On the other hand, the theater industry has succeeded in reaching out to youth. The number of young audiences attending theater has increased, and the trend continues to grow. The results are different when looking at the population with disabilities. They still can't access theaters with enough comfort (Brook, 2016).

Most of the audience continues to be people from the higher social classes with an upper academic background or high literacy levels (Brook, 2016). Democratization of theater in every possible sense continues to be the greatest challenge for theater in the London West End.

This can be achieved by a more significant commitment to work with the communities and give opportunities to create new productions, explore new topics, and form narratives that can talk directly to all those who don't feel represented on stage.

The Continued Cultural and Economic Significance of West End Theater

The theater district in London is the heart of the city and makes the capital the pinnacle of culture in the country. Most cultural venues and activities are concentrated in London and the West End. The theater tours might reach other regions of the country, but they also focus on the West End, where the selection of plays offered is broader and more regular.

Theater is one of the most profitable businesses and generates an intimidating number of £133 million per year.

Over 34 million people attend theatrical shows every year, and that isn't limited to local people but also tourists. According to records, 24% of tourists visiting Great Britain attend shows at the West End (Kingston, 2020). Therefore, it brings revenues and acts as a tourist attraction of its own.

Additionally, theater works as an economic multiplier. It generates over 290,000 job positions, including performers, playwrights, musicians, composers, stage and costume designers, and more. All that without mentioning all the jobs it creates indirectly (Kingston, 2020). For instance, restaurants, other entertainment attractions, parking places, and hotels benefit from the theater.

Nonetheless, the scenario displayed by the pandemic proved these job positions' high level of vulnerability. According to records, 70% of these jobs were at risk. Companies did all they could to hold up their theaters and keep those people covered, but the years after the end of the pandemic were still filled with great uncertainty.

Even through many difficulties, the theater district of the West End has proved to be one of the most vital and dynamic sectors of the economy and the center of the cultural life of Great Britain.

Conclusion

Theater in the West End has proved to be rooted in the very bones of London and, along with the city itself, has earned a place in the history of the world. London theater was the heart of the deepest cultural movements and was the epicenter of political and social changes. It has been encouraged and feared by those in power and valued by people of all social classes and backgrounds. The theater is a space where human nature is explored.

Past and present are blended beyond the logic of time and space. Stories told on stages have been seen by people in this century and centuries before. In the venues concentrated in the West End, people can attend shows of all styles and genres—*The Woman in Black, The Phantom of the Opera, The Mousetrap, The Lion King*, and so many others. This isn't just show business. This is the factory of global culture. This is the place where our art begins.

The West End remains a mixture of modernity and tradition, helping make Western culture what it is. Theaters built at the beginning of the 20th century are being transformed to host the innovations of the new millennium with

Conclusion

their new plays and audiences. It is the world where many worlds can exist. A place that continues to evolve to make room for everybody and to make everybody feel welcome. It is the place where everyone belongs. The West End helped craft the world we live in.

While the West End is busy keeping pace with modernity and its shaking changes, it continues pushing history forward. It is the place of avant-garde theater, performing arts, and inspiration. The future is imagined and created in the West End before it becomes a reality.

For over five centuries, the London West End has been an essential part of the city's life and is vital to the country. It became the cultural capital of the world. Despite the competition with Broadway, the other pinnacle of theater, both theatrical districts have worked together to make performing arts thrive and build a dynamic and fantastic entertainment industry.

The West End and the twists it has come through all these years are clear evidence of what we are as human beings. We are creativity, imagination, reason, and emotion. We embrace life, even in the darkest moments, and we aren't afraid to look reality in its eyes because we are powerful enough to change it. That's what we all learn from the West End's history. That's why we love theater and why theater will live forever.

References

Ballan, D. (2023, May 25). *Charles Dickens and his impact on Victorian society: Understanding the power of literature.* English Plus Podcast. https://englishpluspodcast.com/charles-dickens-and-his-impact-on-victorian-society-understanding-the-power-of-literature/

Barker, C., Izenour, G.C. & Bay, H. (2020, December 3). *Theatre.* Encyclopedia Britannica. https://www.britannica.com/art/theater-building

Bawcutt, N. W. (2009). Puritanism and the Closing of the Theaters in 1642. *Medieval & Renaissance Drama in England, 22,* 179–200. jstor.org/stable/24322803

Beresford, G.C. (2010, June 15). *Mrs Patrick Campbell 1865 - 1940.* National Portrait Gallery. https://www.npg.org.uk/whatson/display/mrs-patrick-campbell

Best, E.W., Campaspe, L. & Best, M. (2002, March 19). *The Blackfriars Theatre.* Luminarium.org. https://www.luminarium.org/encyclopedia/blackfriars.htm

Bevington, D., Spencer, T. & Brown, J.R.. (2023, July 3). *William Shakespeare.* Encyclopedia Britannica. https://www.britannica.com/biography/William-Shakespeare.

Bilotti, K., Halpern, J., McClure, M. & Slade, M. (n.d.). *Drama in the twentieth century.* British Literature Wiki. https://sites.udel.edu/britlitwiki/drama-in-the-twentieth-century/

Bratton, J. (2014, March 15). *Theatre in the 19th century.* British Library. https://www.bl.uk/romantics-and-victorians/articles/19th-century-theatre

Brook, O. (2016, September 13). *Arts council England analysis of theatre in England.* Arts Council England. https://www.artscouncil.org.uk/sites/default/files/download-file/Analysis%20of%20Theatre%20in%20England%20-%20Final%20Report.pdf

Burgess, E. (2019, April 15). *The rise of McTheatre.* The Boar. https://theboar.org/2019/04/rise-mctheatre/

Carlson, M. (2013). Medieval Street Performers Speak. *TDR* (1988-), 57(4), 86–94. http://www.jstor.org/stable/24584845

Carpintero Díez, G. (2015). *Classical mythology in English Renaissance drama: An analysis of Romeo and Juliet.* https://riull.ull.es/xmlui/bitstream/handle/915/1021/Classical+Mythology+in+the+English+

References

Renaissance+drama+an+analysis+of+Romeo+and+Juliet..pdf;jsessionid=782A3D39497F33AAC76DAA2E06870FBD?sequence=1

Cartwright, M. (2020, June 12). *Elizabethan Theater*. World History Encyclopedia. https://www.worldhistory.org/Elizabethan_Theatre/

Cartwright, M. (2022, February 22). *Charles II of England*. World History Encyclopedia. https://www.worldhistory.org/Charles_II_of_England/

Cash, J. (2021, December 28). 25 *Powerful Ibsen plays*. Theater Links. https://theatrelinks.com/henrik-ibsen/#google_vignette

Charles Kean. (n.d.). *National Portrait Gallery*. https://www.portrait.gov.au/people/charles-kean-1811#:~:text=Charles%20Kean%20(1811%2D1868),at%20Covent%20Garden%20in%201838

Critical essays the Renaissance theater. (n.d.). Cliffs Notes. https://www.cliffsnotes.com/literature/d/doctor-faustus/critical-essays/the-renaissance-theater

Daileader, P. (2017, December 1). *What happened to Britain after the Romans left?* Wondrium Daily. https://www.wondriumdaily.com/britain-after-the-romans-left/#:~:text=There%20was%20a%20great%20spread,Britain%20and%20known%20as%20Cerdic

Davies, H.A., Tate, A. & Gardner, H. (2023, August 7). *T.S. Eliot*. Encyclopedia Britannica. https://www.britannica.com/biography/T-S-Eliot

Davis, P. (n.d.). *Best of times: The theater of Charles Dickens*. http://web-static.nypl.org/exhibitions/dickens/works.html

Davis, T. C. (1990). The Independent Theatre Society's Revolutionary Scheme for an Uncommercial Theater. *Theatre Journal*, 42(4), 447–454. https://doi.org/10.2307/3207721

Demographia. (n.d.). *Greater London, inner London population and density history*. http://www.demographia.com/dm-lon31.htm

Dickson, A. (2018, June 21). *An introduction to 18th-century British theatre*. British Library. https://www.bl.uk/restoration-18th-century-literature/articles/18th-century-british-theatre

DiGeorge, P. (2012, February 2). *London Theatre during WWII*. Liberty Lady. https://libertyladybook.com/2012/02/02/london-theatre-during-wwii/

Elizabethan Drama. (n.d.). Encyclopedia.com. https://www.encyclopedia.com/arts/educational-magazines/elizabethan-drama

Encyclopaedia Britannica. (2017, June 14). *Naturalism*. https://www.britannica.com/topic/naturalism-philosophy

Encyclopaedia Britannica. (2022, November 22). *John Rich*. https://www.britannica.com/biography/John-Rich

Encyclopaedia Britannica. (2023, February 9). *Samuel Phelps*. https://www.britannica.com/biography/Samuel-Phelps

References

Encyclopaedia Britannica. (2023, June 21). *Puritanism*. https://www.britannica.com/topic/Puritanism

Encyclopaedia Britannica. (2023, June 23). *Charles Kean*. https://www.britannica.com/biography/Charles-Kean

Encyclopaedia Britannica. (2023, August 18). *Laurence Olivier*. https://www.britannica.com/biography/Laurence-Olivier

Encyclopaedia Britannica. (2023, August 31). *The Blitz*. https://www.britannica.com/event/the-Blitz. Accessed 3 September 2023.

English drama and the English civil war. (2019, February 13). Michaelcrowley.blog. https://michaelcrowley.blog/2019/02/13/english-drama-and-the-english-civil-war/

English Renaissance theatre. (n.d.). New World Encyclopedia. https://www.newworldencyclopedia.org/entry/English_Renaissance_theatre

English Renaissance Theatre: History and facts. (n.d.). StudySmarter. https://www.studysmarter.co.uk/explanations/english-literature/literary-devices/english-renaissance-theatre/

English Renaissance Theatre | English Literature. (n.d.). Lumen Learning. https://courses.lumenlearning.com/suny-britlit1/chapter/english-renaissance-theatre/

Eustace, H. & Parke, N.C. (n.d.). *British theatre in World War One*. Stage Beauty. http://www.stagebeauty.net/th-frames.html?http&&&www.stagebeauty.net/th-wartime.html

Exploring West End London in the Industrial Revolution era. (2023, June 25). WestEndUniverse. https://westenduniverse.com/2023/06/exploring-west-end-london-in-the-industrial-revolution-era/

Facts of William Shakespeare during Elizabethan era. (n.d.). Elizabethan Era. https://elizabethanenglandlife.com/william-shakespeare-during-elizabethan-era1.html

Ferguson, S. L. (2001). Dickens's Public Readings and the Victorian Author. *Studies in English Literature, 1500-1900, 41*(4), 729–749. https://doi.org/10.2307/1556204

Fischer-Lichte, E. (2016, September 27). *Innovation and globalization: Interweaving performance cultures*. Critical Stages/Scènes critiques. https://www.critical-stages.org/14/innovation-and-globalization-interweaving-performance-cultures/

Fox, M. (n.d.). *English Restoration Theatre*. Google Arts & Culture. https://artsandculture.google.com/story/hgWxeWzpWkb17Q

Fox, M. (n.d.). *Post Second World War*. Google Arts & Culture. https://artsandculture.google.com/story/post-second-world-war-society-of-london-theatre/MgVxctGLrST93w?hl=en

From Shoreditch to the West End: The Birth Of London Theatre. (2022,

References

August 23). Londonist. https://londonist.com/london/theatre-and-arts/theatre-london-origins-history-elizabethan

Gainsborough, T. (2011, March 11). *1660 – Theatres reopen after 18 year ban*. Look and Learn. https://www.lookandlearn.com/blog/5491/1660-theatres-reopen-after-18-year-ban/

Gay, P. (2016, November 3). *Comedy in the taming of the Shrew*. The British Library. https://www.bl.uk/shakespeare/articles/comedy-in-the-taming-of-the-shrew

Gioia, T. (2022, July 2). *Why did medieval cities hire street musicians as first responders?* The Honest Broker. https://www.honest-broker.com/p/why-did-medieval-cities-hire-street

The Globalization of Theatre 1870–1930: An interview with Christopher Balme. (2020, February 11). Cambridge University Press. [Video]. Vimeo. https://vimeo.com/390671442

History in focus: War. (n.d.). Leisure in London WWII. https://archives.history.ac.uk/history-in-focus/War/londonLeisure.html

History of London musicals part one. (2012, March 12). London Theater Direct. https://www.londontheatredirect.com/news/history-of-london-musicals-part-one

History of the West End of London. (n.d.). West End. https://www.westend.com/history-of-the-west-end-of-london/

How has the design of theatre buildings changed over time? (n.d.). Theatres Trust. https://www.theatrestrust.org.uk/discover-theatres/theatre-faqs/172-how-has-the-design-of-theatre-buildings-changed-over-time

Jaramillo, C. & Guichard, A. (2020, May 20). *The history of British Theatre | English Theatre History*. Theater Seat Store. https://www.theaterseatstore.com/blog/english-theatre-history

Joan Littlewood. (n.d.). The British Library. https://www.bl.uk/people/joan-littlewood#:~:text=Joan%20Littlewood%20(1914%E2%80%932002),believer%20in%20theatre%20and%20community

Judi Dench | Our Heritage. (n.d.). Open Air Theatre. https://openairtheatreheritage.com/actors/judi-dench/VTeSqyYAACYAQ_To

Kay, W.D. (1995). *Comical satire and the war of the theatres*. In: Ben Jonson. Literary Lives. Palgrave Macmillan, London. https://doi.org/10.1007/978-1-349-23778-4_4

Kent, R. (2021, July 8). *Theatrical influence in the lighting of architecture*. LinkedIn. https://www.linkedin.com/pulse/theatrical-influence-lighting-architecture-kent-leed-ap-assoc-aia/

Kinney, A.F. (2004). *A companion to Renaissance drama*. Blackwell Publishing. Lewis, P. (n.d.a). *Anton Chekhov*. Yale University. https://campuspress.yale.edu/modernismlab/anton-chekhov/

References

Lewis, P. (n.d.b). *George Bernard Shaw*. Yale University. https://campuspress.yale.edu/modernismlab/george-bernard-shaw/#:~:text=The%20Irish%2Dborn%20playwright%20and,%2C%20and%2C%20most%20famously%2C%20Pygmalion

Lewis, P. (n.d.c). *August Strindberg*. Yale University. https://campuspress.yale.edu/modernismlab/august-strindberg/

Lewis, P. (n.d.d). *Gordon Craig*. Yale University. https://campuspress.yale.edu/modernismlab/gordon-craig/

Literature Guide. (2020, July 30). *War of the theatres | The war of the theatres in English literature*. [Video]. YouTube. https://www.youtube.com/watch?v=uVjCZqZyKsk&t=542s

London's oldest theatres in Nostalgic London. (n.d.). The 500 Hidden Secrets. https://www.the500hiddensecrets.com/united-kingdom/nostalgic-london/culture/theatres

London's Roman Amphitheatre. (n.d.). City of London. https://www.thecityofldn.com/directory/londons-roman-amphitheatre/

Lutyens, D. (2018, January 23). *A brave new world of theatre design*. https://www.bbc.com/culture/article/20180122-how-theatre-design-has-become-flamboyant-and-flexible

Marcus, S. (2012). Victorian Theatrics: Response. Victorian Studies, 54(3), 438–450. https://doi.org/10.2979/victorianstudies.54.3.438

Marks, T. (2020, August 14). *The tea-rific history of Victorian afternoon tea*. The British Museum. https://www.britishmuseum.org/blog/tea-rific-history-victorian-afternoon-tea

Maunder, A., Gardner, V., Kelly, V. (2015). *British theatre and the Great War 1914-1919*. Academia.edu. https://www.academia.edu/15512628/British_Theatre_and_the_Great_War_1914_1919

Medieval drama: Meaning, examples and origin. (n.d.). StudySmarter. https://www.studysmarter.co.uk/explanations/english-literature/literary-devices/medieval-drama/

Moravcevich, N. (1970). Chekhov and naturalism: From affinity to divergence. *Comparative Drama*, 4(4), 219–240. http://www.jstor.org/stable/41152534

Nicol, D. (n.d.). *What was the Newington Butts playhouse?* Henslowe's Diary ... as a Blog! http://hensloweasablog.blogspot.com/p/what-was-newington-butts-playhouse.html

Nunn, T., Eliot, T.S., Webber, A.L. & Cartwright, C. (n.d.). *Cats the Musical*. Theater Bookings. https://www.theatrebookings.com/london-musicals/cats#description-tab

Obermajerová, K. (2011). *The Elizabethan and Jacobean history play: Genre revisited*. Masaryk University Faculty of Arts. https://is.muni.cz/th/

References

byqbl/Diplomova_prace.pdf

Offord, S. (2017, March 1). *A history of Oscar Wilde in three plays*. V&A. https://www.vam.ac.uk/blog/news/a-history-of-oscar-wilde-in-three-plays

Oklahoma! (n.d.). Oklahoma Historical Society. https://www.okhistory.org/publications/enc/entry.php?entry=OK090

Pattison, P. (n.d.). *The Roman invasion of Britain*. English Heritage. https://www.english-heritage.org.uk/learn/story-of-england/romans/invasion/

Platt, L., & Becker, T. (2013). Popular musical theatre, cultural transfer, modernities: London/Berlin, 1890-1930. *Theatre Journal*, 65(1), 1–18. http://www.jstor.org/stable/41819819

Playfair, G.W. (2023, May 11). *Edmund Kean*. https://www.britannica.com/biography/Edmund-Kean

Rea, K.G. (2023, August 9). *Western theatre*. https://www.britannica.com/art/Western-theatre.

Realism and naturalism theatre conventions. (n.d.). The English Professor. https://theenglishprofessor.in/realism-and-naturalism-theatre-conventions/

Restoration: Music in the seventeenth and eighteenth centuries. (n.d.). Oxford History of Western Music. https://www.oxfordwesternmusic.com/view/Volume2/actrade-9780195384826-div1-03010.xml

Revenge tragedy of Elizabethan era - English drama. (n.d.). Literature Analysis. https://www.englishliterature.info/2020/10/elizabethan-revenge-tragedy.html

Rolle, E. (2015, May 7). *John Gielgud and John Perry*. Live Journal. https://elisa-rolle.livejournal.com/2060641.html

Ross, D. (n.d.). History of London - Roman London. Britain Express. https://www.britainexpress.com/London/roman-london.htm

Russell, D. (1997). *Popular music in England 1840-1914: A social history*. Manchester University Press. https://books.google.com.ar/books?id=n3PHdGaUqIkC&pg=PA11&lpg=PA11&dq=tear-jerkers+performances+at+tea-rooms+victorian+era&source=bl&ots=-H4vDaPTnu&sig=ACfU3U3AcYKUmKkqAHb8NMic3rfFvDdgWw&hl=es&sa=X&ved=2ahUKEwi_5s6xvYqBAxXjqZUCHU3jAQoQ6AF6BAgvEAM#v=onepage&q=tear-jerkers%20performances%20at%20tea-rooms%20victorian%20era&f=false

Sartika, E. (2016, March 5). *Restoration theater*. English Language Teaching. https://endangsartika17.wordpress.com/2016/03/05/restoration-theatre/

Shakespeare's career. (n.d.). Shakespeare Birthplace Trust. https://www.shakespeare.org.uk/explore-shakespeare/shakespedia/william-shake

References

speare/shakespeare-career/#:~:text=Shakespeare%27s%20reputation%20was%20established%20in,plays%20was%20actually%20the%20first

Shakespeare's history plays: Historical plays by Shakespeare. (n.d.). No Sweat Shakespeare. https://nosweatshakespeare.com/plays/types/history/

Steinbach, S. (2023, August 27). *Victorian era*. Encyclopedia Britannica. https://www.britannica.com/event/Victorian-era

Soergel, P.M. (n.d.). *Theater in the Later Middle Ages*. Encyclopedia.com. https://www.encyclopedia.com/humanities/culture-magazines/theater-later-middle-ages

Statista. (2023, May 16). *Longest running West End productions London 2022*. https://www.statista.com/statistics/690189/longest-running-west-end-productions-uk/

Symes, C. (2023, February 20). *How towns grew in the Middle Ages*. Wondrium Daily. https://www.wondriumdaily.com/how-towns-grew-in-the-middle-ages/

The English Renaissance. (n.d.). Poetry Foundation. https://www.poetryfoundation.org/collections/154826/an-introduction-to-the-english-renaissance

The Restoration. (n.d.). Royal Museums Greenwich. https://www.rmg.co.uk/stories/topics/restoration

Theatre's digital age. (n.d.). Economist Impact. https://impact.economist.com/projects/beyondthespotlight/theatre-ei-article/

Theatres in Victorian London. (2022, March 20). The Victorian Web. https://victorianweb.org/victorian/mt/theaters/pva234.html

Thomas, D. (2014, March 3). *The 1737 Licensing Act and its impact*. In: Julia Swindells, and David Francis Taylor (eds). The Oxford Handbook of the Georgian Theatre, 1737-1832. https://doi.org/10.1093/oxfordhb/9780199600304.013.015

Trumbull, E. (2009, September 9). *Introduction to theater realism*. Northern Virginia Community College. https://novaonline.nvcc.edu/eli/spd130et/realism.htm

Types of Productions. (2007). *Stars of the Edwardian Stage*. Stage Beauty. http://www.stagebeauty.net/th-forms.html

V&A. (n.d.). *Music hall and variety theatre.* https://www.vam.ac.uk/articles/music-hall-and-variety-theatre#slideshow=15664669&slide=0

V&A. (n.d.). *The story of theatre*. https://www.vam.ac.uk/articles/the-story-of-theatre#:~:text=Britain%27s%20first%20playhouse%20%27The%20Theatre,the%20Earl%20of%20Leicester%27s%20household

Vickery, A. & Greig, H. (2022, June 26). *The rise of the West End: London, the season and metropolitan shopping*. Embodied Sociabilities. [Video]. YouTube. https://www.youtube.com/watch?v=5ebzP-qaoLo

References

Who was John Webster | The Duchess of Malfi | Royal Shakespeare Company. (n.d.). Royal Shakespeare Company. https://www.rsc.org.uk/the-duchess-of-malfi/about-the-play/who-was-john-webster

Wiegand, C. (2022, July 21). *London's West End gets first purpose-built theatre in 50 years*. The Guardian. https://www.theguardian.com/stage/2022/jul/21/london-west-end-new-theatre-sohoplace

The world's longest running play in the West End. (n.d.). The Mousetrap Official Site. https://uk.the-mousetrap.co.uk/history/

About the Author

Isaac Miller is a theater nerd who did his own fair share of stage productions when he was in high school and college. While he spends his days in the hustle and bustle of New York City, he spends his nights behind the keyboard, writing down all the things he wants others to know about theater.

On the nights he can't be found behind a computer screen he can be found in the audience of a local stage production.

facebook.com/isaacqmiller

Also by Isaac Q. Miller

How Broadway Became Broadway: The History of the Musicals & Shows that Created the Iconic Street

Join my newsletter to be first the first to know about upcoming new books by scanning the QR code or clicking HERE